Forgive, Love, Renew

A Guide to Unburdening the Heart

Buhlebethu S. Mpofu

An Imprint of Sulis International Press
Los Angeles | Dallas | London

FORGIVE, LOVE, RENEW: A GUIDE TO UNBURDENING THE HEART
Copyright ©2025 by Buhlebethu S. Mpofu. All rights reserved.

All rights reserved. No part of this book may be reproduced in any form or by any means without the prior written consent of the Publisher, excepting brief quotes used in reviews.

ISBN (print): 978-1-958139-65-3
ISBN (eBook): 978-1-958139-66-0

Published by Keledei Publications
An Imprint of Sulis International
Los Angeles | Dallas | London

www.sulisinternational.com

Contents

Introduction 1
Part One Understanding the Root Cause.....................5
1. How The Story Began 7
2. Dealing with Inner Pain 23
3. Stages of Forgiveness 43
Part Two Correcting the Misconceptions 57
4. What Forgiveness is Not...59
5. What Self-Love Is Not...67
6. Self-Love: Won, Not Bought!..................................79
7. Embracing Empathy 91
Part Three Winning The Battle....................................105
8. Leaving The Past Behind......................................107
9. Mindset and Personal Growth 119
10. Winning Your Love..133
11. Power Of Positive Confession 147
12. Grasping The Mindfulness and Meditation Advantage 159
13. Self-Acceptance; A Pathway to Self-Love and Forgiveness 171
14. The Role of Self-Love and the Psychology of Shame 179
Conclusion...193

Introduction

In the intricate tapestry of life, we've all encountered moments of bitterness and offence, wounds inflicted by the careless words or actions of others. Perhaps it was the relentless criticism of parents during our formative years, the betrayal of a colleague who claimed credit for our hard work, the heartache of discovering a partner's infidelity, or the agony of abuse from someone once trusted and cherished: each painful chapter, a testament to the complexities of human relationships and the fragility of trust. As we navigate the labyrinth of our past, we're confronted with a choice: to cling to the shadows of resentment or to embrace the light of forgiveness. The weight of unforgiveness, a burden too heavy to bear, shackles the soul and stifles the spirit. When we harbour bitterness, we sow the seeds of our suffering, reaping a harvest of anguish and despair. To forgive is not to condone or forget the pain inflicted upon us, but to release ourselves from its suffocating grip. It is to relinquish the power that others hold over our emotions and reclaim sovereignty over our hearts. In the act of forgiveness, we find liberation—a pathway to healing and inner peace.

It is not only the wounds inflicted by others that threaten to ensnare us, but also the scars we inflict upon ourselves. Many are haunted by the spectre of past mistakes, consumed by regret and self-loathing. But to wallow in the quagmire of self-hatred is to deny ourselves the chance of redemption. The immutable and unyielding past offers no solace for those who seek to rewrite its pages. And so, we must learn to make peace with our past and accept our flaws and failings with humility and grace, for it is only through self-forgiveness that we can truly move forward, unencumbered by the weight of our transgressions. In the words of the apostle Paul,

> *Recompense to no man, evil for evil. Provide things honest in the sight of all men. If possible, as much as lieth in you, live peaceably with all men. Dearly beloved, avenge not yourselves, but rather give place unto wrath: for it is written, Vengeance is mine; I will repay, saith the Lord. Therefore, if thine enemy hunger, feed him; if he thirsts, give him drink: for in so doing thou shalt heap coals of fire on his head. Be not overcome by evil but overcome evil with good. (Romans 12: 17-21)*
>
> *Ultimately, not vengeance sets us free but love and compassion. So, let us cast aside the shackles of bitterness and embrace the transformative power of forgiveness, for it is through forgiveness that we find redemption and reclaim our humanity.*

Forgiveness is often misrepresented as simply forgetting or minimising the pain one has endured. However, such assertions fail to acknowledge the complexity of human emotions and the lasting impact of past experiences on the psyche. How can one erase the memory of pain when it is etched into the very fabric of their being? Furthermore, the notion that forgiveness necessitates restoring previous relationships is misguided and insensitive. It disregards the validity of one's emotions and undermines the significance of boundaries in interpersonal dynamics. True forgiveness does not demand reconciliation; it offers liberation from the shackles of resentment and bitterness. Despite the prevalent misconceptions surrounding forgiveness, it remains an attainable and transformative journey. Individuals can alleviate psychological burdens and reclaim agency by cultivating self-love and embracing forgiveness. Through forgiveness, the path towards healing and personal growth becomes illuminated, paving the way for a more fulfilling existence. Indeed, the benefits of forgiveness extend far beyond emotional well-being. By releasing grudges and embracing compassion, individuals can foster deeper connections with others and cultivate a greater sense of empathy. In doing so, they free themselves from resentment and contribute to creating a more harmonious and compassionate world.

Forgiveness is not a single act but a continuous process of self-discovery and acceptance. It requires courage, resilience, and a willingness to confront past traumas head-on. However, the rewards far outweigh the challenges, as forgiveness opens the door to inner peace, personal growth, and authentic self-love. As you begin the process of forgiveness and self-love, take time to show yourself patience and understanding. The journey may not always be easy, but each small step forward brings you closer to living a more joyful and fulfilling life. Along the way, we'll explore practical ways to help you grow, transforming how you connect with yourself and others.

Part One
Understanding the Root Cause

1. How The Story Began

"Your thoughts, the way you think is the most powerful influence in your life."
—*Debasish Mridha*

In our minds lies a formidable force: our mind power. This intrinsic ability, coupled with our imagination, is key to shaping our destinies. It can sculpt success or failure, happiness or sadness, and either unveil opportunities or impose limitations upon us. What we choose to nourish our minds ultimately determines our lives' trajectory, influencing our perceptions and colouring our outlook on the world. Despite our best efforts to steer our thoughts in a positive direction, there are moments when life throws us into disarray, leaving us bewildered by the sudden upheaval of emotions.

Picture this: you retire to bed with a heart brimming with contentment, only to awaken the following day engulfed by a suffocating cloud of despair. The weight of negativity bears down upon you, suffusing your thoughts with gloom. You find yourself grappling with a torrent of emotions, each wave crashing against the shores of your consciousness with relentless force. But how did you find yourself ensnared in this labyrinth of despair? The answer lies in accumulating unchecked events woven into your existence's fabric. It may be a seemingly innocuous remark from a friend that now echoes with a newfound sting, or the absence of praise from your boss that leaves you questioning your worth. As you navigate the labyrinth of your mind, you stumble upon memories long buried beneath the sands of time. The spectre of comparison rears its head, casting a shadow over your achievements and magnifying your shortcomings. You find yourself haunted by the ghost of past traumas, their tendrils reaching out to ensnare you in a web of self-doubt and recrimination.

It is akin to living in the shadow of an inner bully, a relentless tormentor that preys upon our insecurities and feeds on our self-hatred. Its whispers are insidious, poisoning our thoughts with notions of inadequacy and unworthiness. But amidst the darkness, there lies a glimmer of hope: the realisation that the first step towards liberation begins with acknowledging the existence of these hateful thoughts. If the relentless onslaught of self-loathing besieges you, take solace in knowing you are not alone. Seek to unravel the tangled threads of your psyche, tracing the origins of these destructive thoughts to their source. Was it a misstep at work that triggered this cascade of self-recrimination? Or perhaps a pang of envy that arose during a seemingly innocuous social gathering? By identifying these triggers, we can begin dismantling the walls of self-hatred brick by brick, paving the way for healing and self-acceptance.

For self-hatred is not merely an isolated phenomenon, but a symptom of a deeper malaise—a downward spiral fuelled by many factors. It is a relentless adversary that thrives in the shadows of our consciousness, preying upon our vulnerabilities with merciless precision. It is also a battle that can be won, provided we arm ourselves with the courage to confront our inner demons and the resilience to emerge victorious. So, as you navigate the labyrinth of your mind, remember this: the journey towards self-love is not easy, but it is worth undertaking. In the crucible of self-discovery lies the promise of redemption, the chance to cast off the shackles of self-doubt and embrace the boundless potential within us all.

Where self-hating thoughts come from

In the intricate mosaic of human emotions and experiences, self-hatred often weaves its tangled threads, ensnaring the hearts and minds of even the most resilient souls. For many, these feelings ebb and flow like the tides, fleeting and transient. For some unfortunate souls, self-hatred takes root deep within their psyche, blossoming into a relentless adversary that knows no respite —a telltale sign of a clinical battle with depression.

The genesis of this internal strife can often be traced back to the formative years of our existence, where the impressions left upon us by our caregivers sculpt the very contours of our identity. Like clay moulded by the hands of a potter, we are shaped by the nurturing embrace or the callous indifference of those who raise us. In the crucible of our early household settings, seeds of self-esteem, compassion, and self-assurance are sown, nourished by the fertile soil of love and acceptance.

Alongside these blossoms of positivity lurk the shadows of negativity, born from the sting of hurtful words and the chill of disapproving glances. For those unfortunate enough to be ensnared in the grip of parental disdain, the echoes of scorn and derision reverberate through the corridors of their consciousness, etching scars upon the tender flesh of their self-perception.

A poignant reminder of this enduring struggle is offered by McLean Hospital in Belmont, Massachusetts, where self-loathing is described as the haunting refrain of "I am just not good." A pervasive sense of inadequacy gnaws at the very core of one's being, whispering tales of unworthiness and failure in the silent chambers of the mind. The insidious nature of self-loathing lies in its subtlety, its ability to cloak itself in the guise of self-reflection while surreptitiously sowing seeds of doubt and despair. Like a malevolent spectre, it lurks in the shadows, casting a pall of self-doubt over even the most mundane activities. With every misstep, it stands ready to pounce, its venomous whispers poisoning the wellspring of self-confidence and drowning out the faintest flicker of hope.

In the depths of darkness lies a glimmer of hope—a beacon of light that pierces through the gloom, illuminating the path towards self-discovery and redemption. It is the realisation that self-loathing is not an immutable truth, but a distorted reflection of one's inner turmoil. This narrative can be challenged and rewritten with courage and determination.

So, as we navigate the labyrinth of our minds, let us remember that self-love is not a destination but rather a journey—a journey fraught with pitfalls and obstacles yet rich with the promise of healing and transformation. With each step forward, let us reclaim our birthright to love and acceptance, casting aside the shackles of self-hatred and embracing the boundless potential within us all.

You are overly critical of yourself

Within our psyche resides an internal critic, a voice meant to guide us away from repeating past mistakes. There comes a point when this voice morphs into a relentless adversary; its once constructive criticisms now serve as daggers aimed at our self-worth. What was intended as a safeguard against failure has become a relentless tormentor, casting a shadow over every triumph and magnifying every misstep.

With each passing moment, this inner critic grows louder, its caustic words echoing through the corridors of our minds like a relentless drumbeat. It becomes a constant companion, lurking in the shadows, ready to pounce upon any sign of weakness or vulnerability. Its whispers of condemnation are like poison, seeping into the fabric of our being and corroding our sense of self-worth. Worst of all, we begin to internalise these negative thoughts, allowing them to dictate our perception of ourselves and our place in the world. We become prisoners of our minds, shackled by the weight of self-doubt and self-loathing. Every success is tainted by the insidious voice of our inner critic, whispering that we are not worthy of praise or recognition. As we spiral further into self-doubt, we find ourselves trapped in a vicious cycle of negativity and despair. The more we listen to the voice of our inner critic, the louder it becomes until its toxic influence threatens to consume us entirely. It is a perilous journey, fraught with pitfalls and obstacles, but one in which we must find the strength to break free. For in the darkness of self-loathing lies the seed of our salvation, the glimmer of hope that whispers a brighter tomorrow. Only by challenging the voice of our inner critic, by refusing to succumb to its relentless barrage of negativity, can we reclaim our sense of self-worth and rediscover the beauty that lies within us all.

Trauma from the past

For many individuals grappling with profound self-hatred, the roots of their anguish are often traced back to harrowing experiences of trauma and adversity. Whether it be the scars of sexual, physical, or emotional abuse or the gaping wounds left by neglect, these individuals carry the weight of their past like a heavy burden upon their shoulders. In the tender years of childhood, when innocence should reign supreme, trauma shatters the fragile veneer of security, leaving behind a gaping void of fear and uncertainty. Unable to make sense of the incomprehensible horrors they have endured, these children fashion narratives of self-blame and inadequacy, seeking solace in the belief that they are unworthy of love and belonging.

Despite their best efforts to bury the pain deep within the recesses of their psyche, it festers like a wound left untended, its tendrils extending into every facet of their existence. Dissociation becomes their refuge, a coping mechanism to shield themselves from the overwhelming onslaught of emotions threatening to engulf them. But the ghosts of trauma are relentless in their pursuit, lying in wait for the slightest opportunity to resurface and wreak havoc upon their fragile psyches. Unprocessed grief, rage, and sorrow linger beneath the surface, festering like a wound left untended, ready to erupt immediately. As the years pass and new wounds are inflicted upon old scars, the pain accumulates, a silent spectre haunting every interaction and relationship. In their desperation to numb the ache within, some turn to self-destructive behaviours or seek solace in harmful pursuits, unwittingly perpetuating the cycle of despair.

In the heart of the shadows, there exists a glimmer of hope—a beacon of light that promises redemption and healing. With compassion and understanding, these wounded souls can unravel the tangled web of their past traumas, forging a path towards self-acceptance and inner peace. It is a journey filled with obstacles and setbacks but offers the promise of freedom from the chains of self-hatred and the start of a new chapter.

No room for errors

A perfectionist typically has no tolerance for error and gives no room for human flaws or limits. At all moments and in all situations, they expect perfection from themselves. Perfectionism damages one's self-esteem and contributes to other mental health issues, such as depression and anxiety. Setting unrealistic expectations usually sets the tone for depression and self-anxiety. Expectations may be in terms of appearance, body weight, relationships, achievements, money, work, education, talents, abilities, personality, or mental health. You believe you're not good enough if you're not perfect, contributing to low self-worth. People who are perfectionists may fear they will never be good enough. Most people often develop a perfectionist mindset to protect themselves from pain and disconnection. It is thought to protect yourself from feeling discomfort by performing flawlessly. However, this anguish may accompany shame, humiliation, isolation, rejection, ridicule, condemnation and other emotions.

Always want to please people

Possessing a generous and caring nature is not inherently detrimental; rather, it serves as a vital attribute in fostering meaningful connections with loved ones. When this kindness veers into excess, becoming a means to bolster one's own self-worth, it morphs into a precarious predicament. In the pursuit of others' happiness, one often neglects one's own, perpetually acquiescing to requests no matter the personal toll. The incessant need to please others leads to emotional exhaustion, a constant state of stress and anxiety.

Bullying

Bullying, an insidious phenomenon prevalent among school-aged children, entails unwelcome and aggressive behaviour, often underpinned by a perceived power asymmetry. This pattern of behaviour, characterised by repetition or the potential for recurrence, encompasses a spectrum of actions—from verbal and physical abuse to social exclusion and cyberbullying. The repercussions of bullying reverberate long after the initial incident, casting a shadow over the mental health and overall well-being of all parties involved: the perpetrators, the victims, and even those who straddle both roles known as bully victims. Furthermore, the spectre of past traumas looms large in everyday interactions, resurfacing unexpectedly through casual conversations or chance encounters. Whether dredged up by a coworker recounting a former workplace ordeal or by a new acquaintance evoking childhood hardship, these memories are poignant reminders of past pain and adversity.

Negative self-concept

Struggling with low self-esteem, a distorted self-image, or a negative self-concept can magnify even minor issues, amplifying them into seemingly insurmountable obstacles. These self-deprecating thoughts often shadow one's perception of events, leading to a pervasive belief in one's inherent inadequacy. Consider a scenario where a joke falls flat amidst friends at a social gathering. Rather than acknowledging the simple truth—that humour can be subjective and not every joke lands—negative self-perceptions may hijack the thought process. Thoughts like "I'm unlikable" or "I'll never fit in" begin to dominate, exacerbating feelings of isolation and unworthiness.

Bad relationships

The genesis of critical inner voices isn't confined to childhood; instead, they can be ignited by experiences throughout life. For instance, relationships—be they romantic, platonic, or professional—can serve as catalysts for the emergence of negative self-talk. Consider a workplace dynamic where a coworker or supervisor habitually undermines your confidence or belittles your abilities. Such interactions can sow seeds of doubt and insecurity, nurturing a toxic inner dialogue that echoes long after the encounter. As the biblical adage warns, *"Be not deceived: evil communications corrupt good manners" (1 Corinthians 15:33),* emphasising the profound influence of interpersonal connections in shaping our inner narrative.

Loneliness

Loneliness encapsulates the emotional void when one's social needs remain unmet. While it is natural for individuals to forge connections within their living and professional spheres, many cannot cultivate meaningful relationships or share their joys and sorrows with those around them. The advent of social media and the frenetic pace of modern life have exacerbated this pervasive sense of isolation. Isolation and loneliness form a symbiotic relationship, each exacerbating the other's effects. Prolonged bouts of loneliness and isolation can exact a toll on both physical and mental well-being. However, it is crucial to differentiate between solitude and loneliness; the former can be a rejuvenating experience, allowing individuals to reflect, refocus, and recharge.

The threshold for solitude varies from person to person, with some craving more "me time" than others. Loneliness can take root when the innate need for social interaction goes unfulfilled over time, affecting individuals across all age groups. Even in the presence of family members, both adults and children may grapple with feelings of loneliness and alienation as others fail to empathise or engage meaningfully. Consequently, the quest for fulfilment may lead individuals to seek solace in external stimuli, perpetuating a cycle of longing and discontent.

Why cannot you forgive yourself?

It is an undeniable truth that, as humans, we're all prone to making mistakes from time to time. Whether it is lapsing in judgment, failures, or falling short of our goals, there are moments when we find ourselves deeply disappointed in our actions. Still, in those instances of self-judgment, granting personal forgiveness can seem like the most challenging thing to do. It is a common thread in human experience to witness moments where self-blame and self-condemnation take centre stage. However, harbouring resentment towards oneself is counterproductive to fostering happiness and well-being. Some individuals grapple with self-forgiveness, clinging to feelings of guilt as a form of self-punishment. Refusing to forgive oneself can inadvertently reinforce a cycle of negative behaviour and perpetuate feelings of unworthiness.

This struggle with self-forgiveness is pronounced in individuals with narcissistic tendencies or idealistic outlooks. Narcissists, characterised by an inflated sense of self-worth and an insatiable need for validation, often find it challenging to acknowledge their fallibility. Instead, they deflect blame onto others or concoct rationalisations to shield their fragile self-image from scrutiny. In their pursuit of preserving an idealised self-perception, admitting mistakes becomes anathema, perpetuating a cycle of self-condemnation and denial.

Prefer to live in denial

Denial is a psychological defence mechanism that shields oneself from confronting uncomfortable realities, thereby alleviating anxiety. When entrenched in denial, individuals consciously reject acknowledging their emotions and the truth of a given situation. Individuals seek solace in the illusion of normalcy by steadfastly refusing to accept and embrace the reality of events unfolding in their lives. In some instances, initial bouts of short-term denial may offer a temporary respite, allowing individuals to gradually acclimate to distressing or challenging circumstances. However, this coping mechanism proves detrimental in the long run, as it fosters a persistent aversion to confronting brutal truths. By steadfastly denying reality, individuals inadvertently stifle their growth and hinder their ability to navigate adversity effectively.

Moreover, the repercussions of denial extend beyond the individual, as they inadvertently deny others the opportunity to challenge or address the situation at hand. By clinging to denial, individuals deceive themselves and deprive others of the chance to offer support or guidance in navigating challenging circumstances.

How does self-hate present?

The manifestation of self-hate varies from individual to individual, each bearing its unique imprint. Some wear their self-loathing like a tattered cloak, evident in the relentless barrage of negative self-talk, the palpable neglect of self-care, and the haunting spectre of depression that looms overhead. For others, the contours of self-hatred are more elusive, cloaked beneath layers of self-sacrifice and unwavering altruism. They are the ones who shun the camera's lens, forever casting themselves as supporting actors in the theatre of life, where their needs take a back seat to the demands of others.

The insidious nature of self-hatred often eludes detection, masquerading as rational discourse rather than a cry for help. To those ensnared in its grip, it feels like a logical conclusion drawn from a lifetime of perceived slights and shortcomings. A childhood devoid of friendship morphs into a belief in one's inherent unlovability. At the same time, the scars of past taunts etch themselves deep into the psyche, distorting perceptions of self-worth and acceptance.

Though fleeting for some, for others, self-hate becomes an unwelcome lodger, a permanent resident in the corridors of despair. Flashbacks to long-forgotten encounters with bullies serve as painful reminders of wounds that refuse to heal, while the echoes of their derision reverberate through the caverns of the mind, feeding the voracious appetite of the inner critic. Nevertheless, within the darkness, a glimmer of hope emerges: the recognition that acknowledgement is the first step toward liberation. By peeling back the layers of self-loathing, one can begin to unravel the tangled web of triggers that perpetuate its grip. Whether it be a misstep at work or a pang of envy at a friend's success, each trigger offers a roadmap to understanding and transcendence.

2. Dealing with Inner Pain

"Your pain is the breaking of the shell that encloses your understanding."
—Kahlil Gibran

Are you grappling with being adrift and hollow, or do you sense yourself inching towards healing from the turmoil? Many of us have navigated similar waters at some point in our journey. Experiencing emotional anguish or feeling lost can sometimes overwhelm us, seeming beyond our capacity to influence. Surrendering to our sorrow only compounds the risk. Regardless of the origins of our inner turmoil, summoning the strength to confront it remains essential.

The depths of psychological suffering can permeate various facets of our existence. For some, it takes a toll on their mental well-being, potentially spiralling into depression and anxiety. Hence, why confront your inner anguish? Well, myriad factors can contribute to such distress. Traumatic encounters, like the loss of a loved one, often serve as catalysts for emotional turmoil. However, psychological distress can also stem from a variety of other triggers, as explored below.

Buhlebethu S. Mpofu

Causes of inner pain

Various personal and environmental factors intertwine to sow seeds of emotional turmoil within the confines of the home. These factors encompass tumultuous relationships with partners, family members, or friends, navigating through significant life transitions like divorce or bereavement, and grappling with chronic health conditions. Additionally, facing homelessness or encountering challenges in conceiving a child can exacerbate emotional distress.

Economic hardships, manifested through low income and the struggle to meet financial obligations, further compound these struggles. Moreover, residing in areas devoid of essential amenities and robust infrastructure exacerbates the strain. Finally, grappling with addictions, be it to substances or detrimental lifestyle habits like smoking or overeating, adds another layer of complexity to the emotional landscape.

Transitioning to the realm of work, emotional distress finds fertile ground amidst the daily grind. While a degree of stress can be construed as motivational, excessive strain can sow the seeds of despair. A myriad of factors conspire to cultivate this distress within the workplace. Anxiety over job security and performance, coupled with the burden of prolonged work hours, casts a shadow over professional fulfilment. Inadequate remuneration and poor working conditions further fuel the flames of discontent. The weight of the additional workload exacerbates these challenges, while strained relationships with colleagues and superiors cast a pall over the work environment.

Personality disorder

Personality disorders can precipitate emotional anguish and a pervasive dread of abandonment. Individuals grappling with such disorders often contend with feelings of social incompetence and inadequacy. Manifestations of these disorders encompass a spectrum of signs and symptoms, including unwarranted nervousness, a compromised sense of self-worth, and recurrent experiences of judgment or rejection. Moreover, navigating social settings proves daunting as individuals contend with an underlying unease and an acute fear of being scrutinised unfavourably. This pervasive anxiety often manifests in the avoidance of group engagements and self-imposed social isolation, further exacerbating their sense of detachment and distress.

Underlying results of inner pain

When our thoughts, emotions, or actions linked to emotional distress reach a level where they significantly disrupt our psychological well-being, they can manifest in various ways:

Sadness: This emotion prompts us to retreat and slow down, facilitating the processing of loss and disappointment. If left unaddressed, prolonged sadness can have profound effects on both mental and physical health, potentially indicating an underlying condition that requires medical attention.

Unexpressed Anger: Anger motivates us to defend ourselves against threats and injuries. It also triggers the release of adrenaline, leading to heightened muscle tension and accelerated breathing, which are similar to anxiety responses. However, if unmanaged, chronic anger can lead to lasting physical consequences.

Anxiety: Anxiety compels us to avoid perceived danger, like the instinctual response triggered by anger. The release of adrenaline during anxiety can result in increased startle responses, restlessness, and an inability to relax, contributing to a sense of being constantly on edge.

Shame and Guilt: Shame drives us to conceal aspects of ourselves that may invite disapproval from others. It often thrives in secrecy and is particularly prevalent among individuals struggling with addiction or engaging in behaviours deemed socially unacceptable. Persistent feelings of shame and guilt can eventually manifest as physical symptoms if not addressed appropriately.

In summary, when emotional distress goes unaddressed, it can lead to a range of psychological and physiological challenges, highlighting the importance of seeking support and intervention when needed.

How to deal with inner pain

When we allow our pain to linger unaddressed, it tends to exacerbate our suffering. Thus, it becomes imperative to confront our hurt head-on and consciously choose to relinquish the grip of inner turmoil, enabling us to progress forward. While our individual experiences of pain may vary, it is a shared human condition, with many having traversed similar paths. However, the differentiating factor lies in navigating and managing this pain. Experts emphasise that becoming entrenched in our emotional distress hampers our personal development and growth. Therefore, it becomes pertinent to explore avenues for releasing this inner anguish. If you are curious about methods for alleviating inner pain, I invite you to join me in exploring potential solutions.

Create a positive mantra to counter the painful thoughts

During moments of emotional turmoil, reinforcing positive affirmations can serve as a powerful tool for mental reorientation and upliftment. By consciously redirecting our internal dialogue towards constructive and empowering language, we can effectively navigate challenging situations and emerge from them with newfound resilience.

For instance, consider a scenario where one faces uncertainty after diligently preparing for an exam, but harbours doubt about their performance. Instead of succumbing to negative self-talk and anticipating failure, consciously affirming one's efforts and potential for success can yield transformative results. By consistently reaffirming one's capabilities and envisioning a positive outcome, individuals can cultivate a mindset conducive to growth and progress, ultimately paving the way for a brighter path forward.

Create physical distance

Once you pinpoint the source of your pain or distress, navigating through it becomes more manageable. It is essential to establish boundaries between yourself and whatever triggers your emotional turmoil, whether it is a person or a particular situation. By mentally distancing yourself from these stressors, you can minimise their impact on your well-being. Redirecting your attention towards activities that bring you joy, and fulfilment can also help shift your focus away from negativity. Rather than dwelling on what angers or upsets you, immerse yourself in pursuits that uplift your spirits and promote a sense of positivity.

Be open to people who fill you up

Are you still secluding yourself in your room? Opening up to others can be incredibly beneficial for yourself and those around you. As inherently social beings, humans thrive on connection, and isolating oneself only amplifies feelings of distress. Surrounding yourself with individuals who bring joy, love, and support can be profoundly transformative. While it may seem straightforward, embracing the company of loved ones is a powerful antidote to loneliness and pain. By leaning on the warmth and encouragement of our social circle, we alleviate our sense of isolation and reaffirm the abundance of positivity in our lives.

Master the act of gratitude

Even in times of hurt, there are still moments of positivity to be grateful. Take a moment to compile a list of these blessings, starting with the simple gift of life and the ability to stand on your own two feet. Amidst the darkness, there's a glimmer of hope for a brighter future capable of overshadowing past pains. While it is important to acknowledge negative emotions, it is equally vital to recognise the good in your life. Consider the support of loved ones like your mother, brother, or devoted spouse who stands by you through thick and thin. Reflect on your job's stability, enabling you to meet your basic needs. Take time crafting this list of positives and revisit it whenever negative thoughts resurface, reminding you of the light amidst the shadows.

Let out all your emotions

The weight of unshed tears and the burden of suppressed pain are heavy chains that bind the soul. Why keep it all locked inside? Let the tears flow; the emotions spill forth like a river breaking free from its dam. Bottling up such anguish is akin to poisoning yourself slowly, unaware of the toxins festering within. Scientists attest to the cathartic power of tears, how they purge the body of accumulated stress and toxins, relieving the weary soul. The body rebels against such suppression, manifesting physical symptoms of distress—tightened muscles, altered breathing—serving as a dire warning of the dangers of emotional repression. It is a perilous path, fraught with the risk of chronic pain, digestive woes, and compromised immunity. Instead, embrace the healing balm of tears and, perhaps, seek solace in the shared sorrows of cinematic tales, finding echoes of your struggles mirrored on the silver screen.

Stop playing the tape

In the intricate tapestry of human experience, there exists a wisdom that is often overlooked but carries profound significance: the art of healing before sharing. We will delve into the timeless truth that our stories, though powerful and transformative, should be shared only after we have tended to our inner wounds. Consider this: the heart and mind are not always in sync. There may come a time when you feel that the pain you once harboured has lost its grip on you. The restless nights and the anxious days seem like distant memories. When the need arises to articulate your story and give voice to your experiences, you discover a subtle but insistent tremor within.

This paradox — the sensation of being healed while still feeling the rawness of emotions when revisiting the past — is a testament to the complexity of our emotional landscapes. In these moments, the wisdom of restraint, of allowing ourselves time and space to mend, becomes evident. We explore the notion that sometimes, speaking about our pain prematurely can inadvertently reopen the very wounds we seek to close. The vulnerability that comes with sharing can serve as a trigger, igniting the embers of old sorrows and causing them to blaze anew. Therefore, the age-old counsel to withhold one's story until healing is well underway holds a profound truth.

Here, we find a paradoxical approach to healing and sharing. After the necessary time for self-reflection, emotional processing, and self-care, we can step into the light of our experiences with newfound strength and clarity. The research underscores this approach, revealing that it dissipates the feeling rather than lingers.

We aim to honour this delicate balance between allowing time for the self to mend and preparing to give voice to one's story. It is a process that acknowledges the ebb and flow of emotions, the silent victories, and the gradual recovery. As you read on, you will find the compelling truth that healing before sharing is not just a suggestion, but a profoundly therapeutic strategy rooted in the depths of human psychology and supported by years of research. This process, tried and tested, has the potential to reshape how we approach our narratives and, in doing so, to reclaim the power of our own stories.

Find a new hobby

Amid the tumultuous journey of life, when we navigate through its web of trials and tribulations, there is a perennial need to discover refuge in the simplest of activities. These are the moments when we must actively seek solace, for it is in doing so that we can momentarily escape the weight of our burdens. The pain we carry, whether emotional or physical, can be temporarily forgotten through moments of engagement and immersion in new experiences.

In such times, embarking on a journey of self-discovery becomes essential. As the saying goes, "To forget one's pain, one must be engaged." This is a call to action, an invitation to venture into the uncharted territory of our interests and curiosities. It may be time to unlock that inner explorer within you, open the doors to new possibilities, and delve into hobbies you have yearned to try but never quite found the time for. Imagine, for a moment, the prospect of yoga. It might have been a thought that danced on the periphery of your consciousness, a lingering desire to embrace its calming embrace. Now, envision the tangible step of seeking a trainer and commencing this journey. No matter how small it may seem, such a choice has the power to ignite a profound transformation within you. It is an act of self-compassion, a decision to prioritise your physical and mental well-being.

These pursuits, these hobbies that we hold dear, are not mere distractions; they are the keys to unlocking their remarkable capacity to heal and rejuvenate the human spirit. Each new hobby, each exploration, is a brushstroke on the canvas of your life, adding depth and vibrancy to your experience. As you embark on this journey, remember that it is not merely about the destination, but the process itself. Embracing new interests and passions is a testament to your resilience and commitment to self-discovery.

In the world of hobbies and self-improvement, there is a world of possibilities to explore, and each venture into the unknown has the potential to breathe new life into your existence. So, when the trials of life seem overwhelming, remember that within you lies the power to find solace, heal, and rejuvenate through the simple act of engaging in the hobbies that resonate with your soul.

Permit yourself to forgive

Forgiveness emerges as a cornerstone of healing, an elixir that eases the burdens of our souls. The path to forgiveness is not always straightforward; it often requires a profound understanding of its transformative power and recognising the inherent complexities. In the exploration of forgiveness, we are faced with a pivotal truth: the healing journey cannot be tethered to the actions or words of others. To truly set ourselves free from the shackles of resentment, we must grant ourselves the profound permission to forgive. This is the key to unlocking the gates of our liberation.

The journey begins with the acceptance that not everyone who has caused us pain will offer an apology.

Clinging to the hope of an apology as a prerequisite for forgiveness is a path fraught with stagnation and suffering. Waiting for the elusive "I'm sorry" from those who have wronged us can imprison us in perpetual anguish. Therefore, the first step in embracing forgiveness is an act of self-compassion. It is the decision to unburden our hearts, irrespective of external conditions, and to prioritise our healing.

Forgiveness is a sacred act that grants us the privilege to release the heavy baggage we carry within—guilt, shame, anger, sadness, and the myriad emotions that often consume us in the aftermath of hurt. It is an act of immense courage, not about condoning the wrongs committed, but about setting ourselves free from the unyielding grip of our pain. Within these pages, we journey through the labyrinth of forgiveness, exploring its nuances, challenges, and immeasurable rewards. Through stories, wisdom, and the guiding light of experienced souls, we unravel the profound impact of forgiveness on the human psyche.

In the art of forgiveness, we understand that its power lies in the remarkable ability to restore balance, to mend the tattered pieces of our soul, and to lead us toward the radiant horizon of renewal and transformation. It offers us the freedom to let go and the wings to soar beyond the pain that once held us captive. We celebrate the liberation that comes from forgiving not only others, but ourselves. We acknowledge that the path to forgiveness is unique for everyone, as is the following experience. We stand together, believing that forgiveness is not a gift solely for the transgressor but a profound act of

Embracing mistakes as steppingstones

self-compassion and a testament to the resilience of the human spirit.

It is the imperfections, the stumbles, and the unexpected detours that often weave the most profound stories. Mistakes, far from being pitfalls, are the stepping stones that shape our journey, infusing it with wisdom and experience. Focus on a transformative exploration of the mindset that views mistakes not as failures but as valuable opportunities for growth. Imagine for a moment that you stand at a crossroads, your heart heavy with the weight of an error made. You are not alone in this sentiment; it is a universal experience, for to err is human. What separates those who thrive from those who languish is their mindset in the face of these errors. It is the steadfast belief that mistakes are not to be dreaded but embraced as instruments of progress.

We journey into the heart of this transformative mindset with a sense of purpose. We learn to hold close the understanding that, at any given moment, we did our very best. This notion envelops us in self-compassion, allowing us to forgive ourselves for our fallibilities, for it is in the act of forgiveness, in the gentle acknowledgement that we are only human, that we find the strength to move forward. Throughout these pages, we encounter stories of individuals who have navigated the labyrinth of self-forgiveness and harnessed the power of their mistakes to propel themselves forward. These tales serve as beacons of hope and inspiration, reminding us that, in our imperfection, we are afforded the gift of experience, the raw material for personal growth.

As we explore the profound benefits of this mindset, we unlock the door to self-acceptance and resilience. We unveil the transformation of pain into wisdom and the healing alchemy that turns missteps into mastery. We reveal the tools and techniques that enable us to apply this perspective in our daily lives, forging a path of continuous self-improvement. Embark on a journey of self-discovery and empowerment. It is a journey that revolves around a powerful truth: mistakes are not the end of the road; they are the very road itself. With this perspective as your guide, you can chart a course toward a brighter, more self-assured tomorrow.

Be clear about what you want

There are moments when we must confront the consequences of our actions. Perhaps, in a fleeting moment, you made a mistake, a lapse in judgment that inadvertently subjected another person to suffering. In these profound instances, the weight of responsibility bears down upon us, compelling us to tread a path of introspection and, ultimately, redemption. The first crucial step on this path is contemplating our actions, which demands earnest self-reflection and a profound understanding of the pain we may have caused. It is not merely about acknowledging the error but also about comprehending the depth of its impact on the lives of others. Empathy becomes a guiding beacon, illuminating the emotions of those affected by our actions.

Having traversed this inner landscape, the next question that looms is determining the course of action. Here, the complexity of human experience reveals itself in all its multifaceted glory. It is a moment when the choice is offered, where the path diverges into two distinct directions. One option involves attempting to reconcile, to bridge the divide that separates us from the person we have wronged. It is a choice that embodies the spirit of forgiveness, a quest to rebuild the bonds of trust and understanding that may have been fractured. It is a journey that requires humility, patience, and a genuine desire to make amends.

On the other hand, there may be instances when reconciliation is not feasible, when the chasm is too vast to bridge, and the wounds too deep to heal. In such cases, the alternative is to seek a path of atonement. It is a journey where we strive to alleviate the suffering we have caused, not through reconciliation but through actions that demonstrate a genuine commitment to righting the wrongs. Ultimately, it is in these moments of reflection and decision that our true character is revealed. Whether we choose the path of reconciliation or atonement, the commitment to growth and self-improvement becomes the driving force. In this crucible of choices and self-discovery, we find the opportunity for redemption, a chance to transform our mistakes into lessons and emerge as better, more empathetic individuals on the other side.

Seek professional help

If, despite your most diligent efforts and exhaustive exploration of all available avenues, you continue to grapple with the arduous task of releasing the burden of your painful experiences, you may find yourself in a place where seeking the counsel of a qualified professional becomes not just a consideration, but a necessity. Adopting these strategies and insights independently may leave you feeling overwhelmed and daunted by the prospect of navigating this complex terrain solo. In such moments, the guidance and expertise of a therapist could offer the invaluable support needed to traverse the intricate path of healing and growth, shedding the weight of your past and embracing a brighter, more hopeful future.

How else can you help yourself better manage emotional stress?

Your health is paramount, so you must build yourself up to manage and cope with stress. Therefore, I emphasise that you take care of yourself by all possible means.

- Take a soothing bath and relax before bedtime.
- Consider reading or drinking chamomile tea to unwind.
- Aim for 8–9 hours of quality sleep each night.

- Explore ways to keep your mind and body relaxed for better sleep.
- Adopt a healthy eating lifestyle; seek help from a nutritionist if needed.
- Engage in regular physical activities to improve your health and body composition.

What are the signs and symptoms of emotional stress?

Emotional stress manifests in two main categories: physical and behavioural/mental symptoms.

Physical symptoms include:

- Anxiety, a heavy feeling in the chest, a rapid heart rate, or tightness in the chest.
- Pain or discomfort in the neck, back, or shoulders.
- General body aches and pains.
- Jaw clenching or teeth grinding.
- Intrusive thoughts and excessive worrying.
- Sudden shortness of breath.
- Feeling lightheaded, dizzy, or unsteady.
- Unexplained weight fluctuations due to changes in eating habits.
- Depression.

- Gastrointestinal issues, ranging from diarrhoea to an upset stomach or constipation.
- Sexual dysfunction or disorders.

These symptoms are signals that your body is reacting to emotional stress and should not be ignored.

Behavioural or mental symptoms of emotional stress include:

- Exhibiting heightened emotions or being unusually sensitive.
- Feeling easily overwhelmed or on edge.
- Struggling with decision-making, focusing, or problem-solving.
- Turning to alcohol or drugs to cope with stress.
- Experiencing memory issues.
- Concerns about suicide prevention.

If someone around you appears to be at immediate risk of self-harm, harming others, or suicide, it is essential to act. You may need to ask direct, compassionate questions to assess the situation and offer support. When supporting someone in crisis, follow these key steps to ensure their safety and well-being:

- Pay close attention to the individual and encourage them to express their feelings openly.
- Stay with the person until professional help arrives.

- Contact local emergency services or text a crisis counsellor for assistance.
- Remove any potentially harmful objects or medications to ensure the person's safety while awaiting help.

Your immediate intervention can make a crucial difference in such situations.

3. Stages of Forgiveness

"Someone who does not forgive breaks the bridge over which he must pass."
—George Herber

Understanding the benefits of an action can significantly boost one's motivation to pursue it. In the case of forgiveness, comprehending the advantages you gain from pardoning others can be a powerful catalyst for your willingness to forgive consistently. Forgiveness is pivotal in fostering a content and satisfying life, underscoring the importance of avoiding harbouring unforgiving sentiments. Failure to reconcile with feelings of anger and resentment may lead to adverse effects such as depression and interpersonal conflicts.

Forgiveness is a personal choice, a decision that originates within oneself. While it may not be an immediate cure, it is a transformative tool for personal growth and positive global impact. Recognising that your actions and reactions emanate from within reinforces the notion that forgiveness, albeit challenging, holds immense value. Practising forgiveness liberates one from the shackles of pain, animosity, and suffering. Furthermore, extending forgiveness aids in achieving even the most immediate and practical goals.

One's perception of forgiveness significantly influences their beliefs and decisions. Striving to forgive others diverts energy away from harmful and distressing thoughts, creating a more fulfilling life. Learning the art of forgiveness doesn't just benefit; it proves invaluable. The question arises: How does one truly forgive? This section delineates four stages of forgiveness, providing a pathway to navigate issues, irrespective of their magnitude. Commencing with more minor matters and gradually progressing can aid in understanding the concept better. It is advisable not to forgive someone likely to cause further harm until you have gained ample experience and knowledge in forgiving others.

Stage 1: Acknowledge the harm

In the first stage of healing and forgiveness, it is essential to confront the pain that has been inflicted upon you. This initial step is crucial in the journey toward emotional recovery and ultimately forgiving who wronged you. To illustrate this, let's delve into the story of John and Belinda. "You look out of shape," John mocked Belinda. His words were like a dagger to her heart, piercing her self-esteem and causing emotional turmoil. Despite her hurt, Belinda smiled, concealing her genuine emotions beneath a facade of composure. She didn't reveal the depth of her anguish to John, opting instead to mask her pain with a false sense of well-being. It is important to emphasise that when acknowledging the harm, one should not downplay or excuse the wrongdoing committed by the offender. Instead, it is vital to face the reality of the situation head-on. This requires a deliberate and introspective approach. One effective method for achieving this is maintaining a diary, a confidant in which you can honestly document your feelings, thoughts, and experiences.

Keeping a diary is an organising tool for your emotions, providing a structured outlet to navigate the complex web of emotions that often accompanies hurt and betrayal. It enables you to accept the truth without compromise, allowing you to confront your feelings and face the pain inflicted upon you. Furthermore, writing a letter to the offender, although it may not be intended for actual delivery, can be therapeutic. This letter processes your emotions, enabling you to express your feelings and offer forgiveness. It allows you to confront the wrong that has been done to you and aids in shaping the way you think and feel about the situation.

Acknowledging the harm is a pivotal first step towards healing and forgiveness. It entails facing the emotional wounds inflicted by others without minimising or excusing their actions. Keeping a diary and writing letters to the offender are valuable tools in this process, helping you navigate the tumultuous waters of hurt and ultimately find a path towards forgiveness and emotional restoration.

Stage 2: Write down your happy feelings about the situation

We all encounter situations where someone's actions or words can deeply wound us. It is natural to experience a surge of emotions in response to these events, typically anger, resentment, or regret. The critical thing to remember is that these feelings are not wrong; they are a human reaction to the wounds we have suffered. To effectively navigate these emotional landscapes, it is imperative to confront them head-on and healthily express them.

Once you have identified the offence, it is time to delve deeper into your emotional response by documenting how it affected you. This cathartic process liberates the emotions that may be festering within. In this written exercise, recount the events leading up to the offence as clearly and honestly as possible. This narrative will serve as a testament to your experience, helping you better understand the situation.

Next, it is essential to compile a list of your current emotions about the situation. In this endeavour, honesty is paramount. Strive to capture your raw, unfiltered feelings, not the socially acceptable responses you might think you should have. Confronting these genuine emotions opens the door to healing and growth. Remember that moving forward begins with acknowledging your current emotional state. You cannot progress from where you wish to be; progress starts from where you currently stand. In recognising and expressing your true feelings, you empower yourself to move forward from a place of authenticity and self-awareness. This is the second stage of healing and growth, a vital step to finding peace and resolution.

Stage 3: Write down the benefits you will gain from forgiving

Forgiveness often appears daunting, far more formidable than clutching onto the familiar comforts of bitterness and resentment. It is an innate human desire to seek justice for the wrongs we have endured, and it is tempting to believe that clinging to our grudges and grievances is the surest path to obtaining that elusive sense of retribution. Paradoxically, the most arduous journeys often yield the most valuable rewards.

Consider this inevitable truth: Forgiveness will become integral to your life's narrative, recurring as frequently as the seconds tick away on the clock. Whether it be an act required once a month, a weekly endeavour, or a daily ritual, the decisions you make concerning forgiveness or its absence will invariably leave an indelible mark on the canvas of your existence. As you contemplate the profound advantages that forgiveness bestows upon those who embrace it, remember that this transformative process is not only an act of compassion but also a profound act of self-preservation. Through forgiveness, you unlock the doors to a brighter, more harmonious future, where the echoes of the past no longer hold sway over your destiny.

Stage 4: Promote peace

Forgiveness stands as a beacon of hope, a bridge toward serenity. In forgiveness, we uncover the key to unlocking the doors of tranquillity, ushering in harmony within ourselves and the world around us. When we cannot forgive those who wronged us, we inadvertently thrust ourselves into perpetual conflict. This is a war of our own making that plays out within the chambers of our hearts and the corridors of our minds. In this internal battleground, we wage ceaseless battles, defending the fortress of our innocence with fervour. This relentless defence, however, swiftly exacts its toll, sowing the seeds of negativity into every aspect of our lives, irrespective of the scale of the transgression. Engaging in quarrels and conflicts with those who traverse the path of our existence is a treacherous endeavour. It is a corrosive force that erodes the foundations of our relationships, exacting a heavy toll on our time, energy, and, perhaps most significantly, our happiness. The collateral damage extends to the harmony we share with ourselves, disturbing the tranquil waters of our inner peace. The insidious nature of such conflicts draws us into a never-ending vortex, a self-perpetuating cycle that seemingly has no end in sight. It is a downward spiral, an abyss into which we willingly descend while clutching the shards of our grievances. Ultimately, what do we indeed gain from this unyielding stance of unforgiveness? The answer, quite simply, is loss.

We lose precious time that could have been spent in more meaningful pursuits. We squander our energy in ceaseless battles that yield nothing but exhaustion. We forfeit the happiness that is rightfully ours as it becomes overshadowed by the looming spectre of bitterness. Most tragically, we forfeit the beauty of our relationships, once flourishing gardens now left barren by our refusal to forgive. As we stand at this crossroads of our own making, forgiveness offers us a lifeline. The beauty of forgiveness is in its ability to bestow peace upon us, a peace that transcends the turmoil of our past grievances. Through forgiveness, we cease our internal war and become at peace with ourselves. Here, in this harmonious state, we discover the true treasure that forgiveness affords. We gain more than we ever lose when we choose the path of forgiveness. In embracing it, we find the serenity of a heart unburdened; in that serenity, we discover the profound power of our humanity.

You have more time to build the life you want

Struggling to forgive others can consume your thoughts and energy, leading to a fixation on perceived wrongs, expressing dissatisfaction, and contemplating revenge. This reluctance to forgive holds you back, particularly in today's digital age, where constant access to others' lives amplifies such tendencies. You might continuously monitor old friends or those who have wronged you, investing significant time and energy into these pursuits. This time could be better spent on more productive endeavours. Forgiveness frees you from this cycle, allowing you to focus on your own life and priorities rather than dwelling on the actions of others. You can maximise your time and create a more fulfilling existence by directing your attention towards meaningful relationships and activities. Embracing forgiveness yields numerous benefits, ultimately contributing to the fulfilment of your desired life path. Granting forgiveness offers six distinct advantages:

You Begin to Become More Present in Life

By adopting forgiveness as a practice, you free up time to construct the life you envision and cultivate a greater sense of presence and joy in your daily experiences. Contrastingly, harbouring resentment impedes productivity and distracts from the present moment, causing you to dwell on past grievances rather than engage fully with life. Embracing mindfulness offers many advantages, such as fostering creativity, reducing stress, and minimising regret. Ultimately, it allows you to savour each moment and avoid wasting precious time on unproductive emotions that do not enrich your life.

You Become More Sympathetic

Forgiveness prompts a shift in perspective, fostering empathy and understanding towards others. For example, forgiving someone for betrayal requires recognising their humanity and acknowledging the circumstances that influenced their actions, which may have been driven by confusion, distress, or negativity rather than malice. Viewing individuals with compassion enriches relationships and minimises conflict and negative emotions. Embracing this mindset allows for greater harmony and encourages thoughtful communication, ultimately enhancing personal well-being and interactions with others.

Your Exemplary Act of Forgiveness

Your example holds immense value for many when you extend forgiveness, particularly to those who've wronged you. The person forgiven receives a profound demonstration of genuine compassion and fortitude. This act also ripples positively, affecting the lives of family, friends, and even strangers.

Consider this: I have witnessed individuals forgive others for truly abhorrent deeds, and my admiration for them knows no bounds. Their actions have taught me the essence of standing firm, maintaining fairness, and upholding my moral compass—a lesson of monumental significance. These lessons have unequivocally enriched my life, and undoubtedly, they've impacted others similarly. In essence, practising forgiveness earns the respect of others. They perceive you as a paragon of strength, confidence, and love—qualities they aspire to embody. Consequently, you become someone they seek, enhancing relationships in myriad ways.

Enhanced Health Through Forgiveness

Forgiveness yields remarkable health benefits owing to the robust connection between mind and body. The Mayo Clinic underscores forgiveness as a catalyst for improving the immune system, heart health, and blood pressure while aiding in combating anxiety, stress, and depression. Essentially, embracing forgiveness improves overall health and is a preventive measure against future illnesses. In my personal experiences, witnessing seniors extend forgiveness has been illuminating. The transformation in their health has been profound: the perpetual frowns vanished, worries dissipated, and a newfound ability to laugh and prioritise self-care emerged. Consider a man whose bitterness kept him confined to his home; through forgiveness, he appeared to reclaim years of his life. Suddenly, he stood taller, moved with agility, and exuded a youthful energy previously unseen.

You Earn Self-Respect

It is an interesting paradox — we often believe that clinging to anger upholds our honour and dignity. However, the truth is that it is forgiveness that genuinely enhances our sense of honour and dignity. When you embrace forgiveness, you gaze into the mirror and experience a profound sense of self-worth. You see a resilient individual capable of looking beyond imperfections and the shortcomings of others. It is about mastering life's reins and orchestrating your daily actions, fostering genuine pride and confidence. Conversely, the inability to forgive aligns you more closely with those you resent. When you dislike someone's actions, seeing yourself mirrored in their light leads to self-disdain.

This aspect of forgiveness is among the most visible benefits. As other positive changes unfold, happiness naturally follows suit! You can't help but feel more engaged, purposeful, and content in relationships and towards your future. Life takes on a brighter hue when you release the past, focusing on the present and envisioning what lies ahead. Consider forgiving someone who betrayed your trust. It involves recognising their flaws, acknowledging that, like all of us, they acted from a place where love and enlightenment were lacking. It is crucial to understand that their actions weren't rooted in happiness but in confusion, distress, or negativity. When you grasp this understanding about someone who has caused you pain, you start seeing it as a universal truth applicable to everyone.

Viewing people through compassionate lenses is rewarding. It enhances your ability to relate, enriching your relationships. It steers you away from conflicts and negative emotions, offering a more gratifying alternative to anger and discord. Moreover, it nurtures a heightened sensitivity in your words and thoughts, cultivating a sense of integrity in your actions.

You Become Happier

One of the most evident advantages of forgiveness is the resulting increase in happiness. Happiness naturally follows suit as other positive outcomes unfold, such as heightened activity, clarity of purpose, improved relationships, and optimism about the future. Letting go of past grievances allows for a greater sense of contentment and fulfilment as attention shifts towards the present moment and aspirations for the future.

Affirmation for forgiveness

Action comes naturally when you are on the right path, and forgiveness follows suit. Verbalising and contemplating the right words facilitate the process, recognising that the past is immutable while the future remains open. Focusing on the present becomes essential, as dwelling on past grievances hinders enjoyment and progress. Letting go of past burdens is akin to shedding the weight of a metaphorical monkey on your back, enabling forward momentum. Simultaneously, harbouring bitterness prevents the entry of positive emotions, inhibiting personal growth. Holding on to past hurts only serves to impede progress. Embracing forgiveness liberates both oneself and others from the shackles of resentment. Stagnation in a self-development journey often signals unresolved past issues. Letting go, forgiving, and moving forward are imperative steps towards continued growth. While the past offers valuable lessons, it should not dictate the future trajectory. Taking ownership of one's reactions and decisions empowers individuals to shape their lives consciously. Blaming others relinquishes personal agency, whereas assuming responsibility allows for intentional responses.

Utilising forgiveness affirmations fosters a daily practice of letting go and moving forward. Here are affirmations to nurture forgiveness daily:

I love others as much as I love myself.

- I refuse to take offence to today's wrongs.
- No harm will shatter my spirit today.
- I release all grudges with forgiveness.

There will come a day when you will think about the person who hurt you with a completely different perspective. While you may never fully trust or embrace them again, the weight of anger and bitterness will lighten. Forgiveness is a pathway to personal freedom, not necessarily reconciliation. You can forgive without re-inviting someone into your life. Understanding that forgiveness heals the past while boundaries safeguard the future is crucial. You have the right to protect yourself from further harm, to set limits, and to demand respect. Remember, you don't need validation from someone who once caused you pain.

Part Two
Correcting the Misconceptions

4. What Forgiveness is Not

"Do not let a few minutes of anger and frustration mess the remaining hours of the day."
—*Unknown*

During college, I had a close friend named Lucia, with whom I shared intimate details about our lives. At that time, she was in a relationship with Arthur. On December 25th of our final year, she visited Arthur, and he proposed intimacy, which she declined. Both of us had decided to preserve our dignity and save our most precious gift for our future husbands, even though many of our peers were already sexually active. Regrettably, he disregarded her refusal and forced himself on her. The experience was harrowing and heartbreaking, leaving Lucia deeply hurt and emotionally shaken. This incident led to her developing a profound resentment towards Arthur, ultimately marking the end of their relationship.

Even after Arthur faced legal consequences and was found guilty of rape, Lucia remained upset and angry. However, grappling with forgiveness proved to be a challenge for her. She struggled to reconcile, forgiving someone she once loved and trusted deeply, but who had betrayed that trust and taken advantage of her.

Understanding forgiveness is not always straightforward. When faced with hurtful actions, one may question the possibility of forgiveness. However, as time passes, gaining a better understanding of forgiveness can make the process easier. Many resources discuss forgiveness, but few delve into what forgiveness is not, which is crucial to comprehend. What exactly does forgiveness entail? Should people be forgiven only if they ask for it? Does forgiving someone mean trusting them again? In this writing, I aim to unveil answers to these questions and explore the complexities of the forgiveness journey.

What does forgiveness mean?

Forgiveness is a conscious and intentional decision to release feelings of revenge or retaliation towards someone or a group of people who have wronged you, regardless of whether they deserve your forgiveness. It does not imply allowing the offence to be repeated. Instead, it involves relinquishing bitterness towards a person or a situation. To forgive is to acknowledge that what transpired cannot be changed. It requires ceasing to dwell on it, redirecting your attention, and overcoming any lingering irritation. Doe Zantamata suggests that many individuals mistakenly believe forgiveness entails erasing a hurtful event from memory and resuming life as if nothing happened. However, Zantamata argues that this perspective represents wilful forgetting rather than true forgiveness, and it can potentially lead to remaining trapped in adverse situations. True forgiveness involves letting go of a negative event and moving forward. In essence, forgiving means accepting a particular behaviour without necessarily tolerating it. It signifies that while you forgive someone, it does not equate to approving of their actions. Forgiveness is for your benefit, enabling you to release the burden and live your life as if the harmful event never occurred, protecting yourself from the detrimental effects of resentment.

Should people be forgiven until they ask for it?

One of the most valuable lessons I have learned about conflict resolution is a saying my father often shared with me: "Baby, it takes two people to quarrel." This statement holds as it highlights the necessity of two parties for disagreement or conflict to arise, but it also implies that resolution requires mutual effort. Essentially, both individuals involved must be willing to reconcile for harmony to be restored.

Regarding forgiveness, it is essential to understand that forgiveness primarily benefits the offended party rather than the offender. It is not contingent upon receiving an apology; instead, it allows the individual to release feelings of malice and bitterness, preserving their emotional well-being. True reconciliation may not always be possible if both parties aren't actively engaged. However, letting go of anger and resentment is essential to prevent them from consuming one's peace of mind. For instance, consider the typical scenario of being cut off in traffic. While it is natural to feel frustration in such situations, holding on to that anger only disturbs one's inner peace and fosters resentment. Therefore, it is crucial to recognise when to release negative emotions and prioritise personal well-being over holding on to grudges.

Bringing that anger into your workplace affects your mood for the entire day because you haven't released it. Even if the person who upset you has not apologised, you can still choose to forgive them by releasing the negative emotions associated with their actions. While true reconciliation may not occur without mutual effort, forgiveness involves letting go of resentment and not allowing past events to dictate your future interactions or demeanour. It is important to avoid holding on to grudges and instead be open to letting go of negative experiences. Additionally, forgiveness is a decision rather than a feeling, so waiting for a sense of forgiveness to spontaneously arise may be futile.

Is forgiveness minimising the seriousness of the offence?

In life, we encounter various situations where people may treat us poorly. How we respond to such behaviour is crucial, as it can significantly impact our well-being.

Forgiveness does not diminish the seriousness of an offence. There's a distinction between being accidentally injured and intentionally offended. When someone deliberately hurts our feelings, forgiveness becomes necessary. It is important not to downplay the significance of the offence when someone seeks forgiveness.

If it wasn't a big deal, there's no need for an apology or forgiveness. Forgiveness is reserved for significant transgressions, not trivial matters. If something warrants forgiveness, don't belittle it when asked for forgiveness. Instead, acknowledge the gravity of the situation. Understand that forgiveness doesn't mean pretending you weren't hurt. It is not about wearing a fake smile while suffering internally. Feeling hurt or betrayed by someone's actions is a natural response to betrayal or loss of trust.

Does forgiveness mean condoning the offender?

Many people feel reluctant to forgive because they think that the offender is getting away with the offence or that forgiving the offender will somehow mean accepting the bad behaviour of the offender. When you forgive someone, you relieve yourself from the bitterness you may feel. My friends Charlotte, Jane and Patricia had a lovely time at my house a few years back. Jane talked about how her father molested her from 5 years to 14 years during the conversation. She also mentioned how courageously and beautifully her mother had to forgive their father without sending him to prison, quit the marriage and move on with her life by trying her best to care for her so that she would not be affected by that incident throughout her journey in life. It infuriated Patricia, who talked about how uneasy she felt with what Jane said.

Because she feels that forgiving the wrongdoer is like letting them off the hook so they can continue to harm others, Jane's comment addresses one of the most prevalent misunderstandings about forgiveness. This misunderstanding is that when you forgive someone, you accept and tolerate the wrongdoer. If you forgive, you must ask yourself if you are letting them off the hook for their actions, making what they did to you okay. It is often one of the reasons why many people refuse to forgive someone or something that happened in their past. Please remember this. When you forgive someone, you are not in any way accepting the wrong they did to you. Forgiveness is something that you need to decide to do for yourself. It is eventually not about the other person at all.

When you decide to forgive, you can release yourself from the bondage of bitterness, anger, and accusation and heal yourself from the mental and emotional burdens of your experience. Offering yourself the gift of forgiving people doesn't have to do with the other person and their behaviour towards you. You may be thinking, "How is that possible?" You may think that harmful incidence has to do with the other person's behaviour toward you. After all, they took advantage of you, harmed you and cheated on you in one way or another. It is normal for you to feel hurt by your experience with them, but even though they offended you, you are the one who is responsible for your feelings. It would be best to admit that in this world where we find ourselves, "Pain is inevitable, but suffering is an option."

When you choose to forgive, you decide not to suffer. It is a choice you must make selfishly, for your best interests, and if necessary, without worrying about how it will affect somebody else. Since you can perpetuate the anguish, you can end it. Forgiveness is about releasing yourself from the self-constructed prison of suffering and negativity. Think of it this way: when you're holding a grudge, resentment or anger toward someone else, that person is always living in your consciousness. They are always with you, without them even knowing or being affected. Forgiveness creates growth opportunities and opens the door to new paths forward.

Does forgiveness mean trusting the offender?

If someone betrays you, they don't automatically regain your trust. Early in her relationship with James, Sophia discovered his infidelity. Despite numerous confrontations and denials, James continued communicating with other women despite promising Sophia exclusivity. Their arguments often escalated into physical altercations. Despite her love for James, Sophia eventually ended the relationship after enduring his destructive behaviour for two years. Although James pleaded for reconciliation, Sophia feared the situation would worsen if they reunited. She no longer trusted him, which also meant she no longer loved him, despite the potential for forgiveness over time. Forgiveness doesn't equate to welcoming someone back into your life or heart. In many cases, those who have caused harm shouldn't be trusted again, even if forgiveness is extended.

Repentance should not be a condition for forgiveness, as genuine remorse involves taking full responsibility without guilting the injured party. Trust must be rebuilt over time, demonstrating consistent, trustworthy behaviour. Some individuals harbour self-loathing for their past actions, leading to a lifelong struggle with their conscience. Others may outwardly appear content, but silently suffer from past traumas. Both scenarios highlight the importance of self-forgiveness and the indirect productivity boost from letting go of negativity. Forgiveness allows individuals to move forward without being weighed down by past grievances, ultimately enhancing productivity and well-being.

5. What Self-Love Is Not

"Self-love is not selfishness. It is about setting boundaries, not building walls."
—Unknown

Self-love is not merely a cliché; it is a tangible emotion comparable to the love one feels for a child or a friend, accompanied by a disposition toward self-compassion. It goes beyond mere self-liking; it involves recognising one's core values and character traits and committing to uphold them, especially during challenging times. Values such as kindness, forgiveness, and compassion guide our interactions with others and shape our existence in the world. Self-love encompasses nurturing relationships, establishing healthy boundaries, and fostering personal growth and well-being.

It encompasses one's self-perception, self-treatment, and self-care practices. Imagine how you would behave, speak to yourself, and feel about yourself if you genuinely loved and cared for yourself. While self-love leads to a positive outlook on life, it doesn't mean you always feel good about yourself. It is natural to experience sadness, anger, or disappointment and still love yourself. Self-love is about unconditional acceptance, appreciation, and love for oneself. Regardless of circumstances, it means always choosing to love oneself more.

Self-love is a journey

Truly loving yourself is no easy feat; it is a challenging endeavour. It is natural to question your self-worth during setbacks, but dwelling on such thoughts is unhealthy. Cultivating self-love requires full commitment and dedication, as it is the most potent form of love. No one else can provide us with happiness or love unless we first learn to love ourselves. It is important not to equate self-love with narcissism or excessive ego; it is simply about valuing oneself. Prioritising self-care and well-being is not selfish; it is an essential aspect of self-love. However, self-love doesn't mean always putting oneself first at the expense of others. Despite potential misunderstandings, only you know what is truly best for yourself.

Is self-love selfish?

Selfishness may not be regarded as the most favourable human trait, often earning a negative reputation due to its perceived detestable nature. It is a trait inherent in all individuals to some extent, leading to self-dislike and disdain toward others who exhibit it. However, selfishness serves a necessary purpose for survival, literally and figuratively. Without some degree of self-preservation, one would face dire consequences such as starvation or exposure to the elements.

Throughout our lives, we've been repeatedly taught that selfishness is a reprehensible quality, often associated with hostility. However, life is rarely black and white; it is filled with shades of grey. Selfishness isn't inherently destructive; it exists on a spectrum ranging from minimal to extreme. Not all behaviour labelled as selfish is harmful, contrary to what we've been conditioned to believe. It is essential to understand what self-love is not, including but not limited to:

Self-love is not being egoistical

Indeed, possessing an ego is a common trait; it is something everyone has. However, when left unchecked, it can become problematic. An uncontrolled ego permeates every aspect of one's life, influencing decisions and attitudes, often leading to a sense of victimisation in various situations. Consequently, this can breed feelings of misery.

An unrestrained ego has the potential to deprive individuals of meaningful experiences and distance them from others. It shapes how one navigates life, hindering the ability to cope with adversity or disappointment healthily. Being boastful, arrogant, or excessively self-centred does not indicate self-love; these qualities are unnecessary for genuine self-appreciation. It is crucial to recognise the impact of one's ego on decision-making, as an unchecked ego can have adverse effects. By being mindful of one's ego, individuals can improve their interpersonal relationships and better manage themselves and others. Developing self-awareness regarding the influence of the ego can significantly enhance happiness and overall well-being over time.

Self-love is not thinking that you're never wrong

Self-love involves acknowledging your shortcomings as they arise. It recognises that everyone is prone to making intentional or unintentional mistakes. Believing that you're immune to errors leads to self-criticism. Self-love entails treating oneself with kindness. While regretting mistakes is natural, dwelling on them excessively is counterproductive. Instead, it is essential to glean lessons from mistakes and continue forward.

Self-love is not a luxury

When you need a break, practising self-love could involve simple acts like hydrating yourself with a glass of water, ensuring your kitchen is filled with nourishing foods for upcoming busy weeks, or enjoying quality time with a friend who brings you joy. It also entails recognising when you require additional rest and prioritising a good night's sleep. Self-love may include asserting boundaries with a demanding boss or friend and carving out personal space to prioritise your well-being.

Self-love is not about disregarding your flaws

Self-love does not imply disregarding imperfections; rather, it entails loving yourself despite them. It indicates you care so much about yourself that you want to be, do, and treat yourself better. Maybe you shudder when you think about how much alcohol you have consumed or how much sugar you have consumed. But, because your listening abilities decreased after elementary school, you may always manage to get into arguments with everyone, all the time. You might enjoy things the way they are, and when other people mess with the order and regularity you have established in your life, your heart and mind feel as if they've sunk into chaos; you strive for flexibility but struggle to let go of control.

You may be the type of person who breaches promises to others and yourself. You don't do it to be cruel, flaky, or insensitive; you don't know how to say "no," so you end up saying "yes" to far too many things, and you end up having to be the last-minute canceler. Maybe you're the type of person who constantly complains about their situation while doing nothing to improve it. Or you're blaming others too much for things entirely within your control. Maybe it is something else entirely, but if you're honest with yourself, you don't always appreciate some aspects of your personality — and that's fine.

True self-love entails accepting all the characteristics that make you, well, you. It is about seeing and accepting your flaws as part of being human. It is about accepting that there are aspects of yourself that you may not always like or even adore, but that doesn't mean you should berate or punish yourself for them. Coming to terms with the things you'd instead brush under the rug and finding a means to deal with them while you stand in the light is what self-love is all about. Self-love is about accepting and loving oneself enough to adapt, grow, and learn.

Self-love is not something you have to do alone

Our traditional notions of self-love often centre on solitude. However, finding moments alone has become increasingly uncommon in today's constantly connected world. On the other hand, learning to love yourself might be much easier when you're among a community of like-minded people who can truly appreciate your unique traits and reflect them to you. If you have been trying to love yourself in solitude, it might be time to connect with a supportive group of friends who can show you what you're missing – the little things others notice about you that you never see yourself.

Building self-love

Below are several ways you can achieve total self-love:

Put yourself first

Feeling guilty for prioritising yourself is unnecessary. Women, especially, may often find themselves inclined to prioritise others' needs over their own. While this altruistic behaviour has merits, it should not become a habitual practice that compromises mental and emotional health. It is essential to carve out time for relaxation and self-care. Neglecting to decompress and recharge can lead to excessive stress and strain. Discover activities that help you unwind and dedicate time to them, whether it involves a day spent in bed or a leisurely walk in nature.

Quit comparing yourself with others

When we constantly measure ourselves against others, we risk diminishing our self-worth and undermining our confidence. Comparisons often lead to feelings of inadequacy and dissatisfaction with our own lives. Moreover, the curated nature of social media can exacerbate these feelings, as we are exposed to carefully selected highlights of others' lives, which may not accurately reflect reality. Remember that what we see online is often a polished version of reality, and comparing ourselves to these images can be misleading and detrimental to our self-image. Instead of fixating on others' achievements or appearances, focus on your journey and progress. Celebrate your strengths, accomplishments, and unique qualities, recognising that everyone's path is different and success is subjective. Practising gratitude for what you have and cultivating self-compassion can also help counteract feelings of inadequacy. Acknowledging and appreciating your worth and accomplishments can foster a greater sense of self-love and acceptance.

Take it one day at a time

Growth and change are gradual processes, and nurturing your sense of self-worth is no exception. Adopting a mindset of patience and persistence is essential, recognising that meaningful progress takes time. Each day presents an opportunity to celebrate minor triumphs and significant milestones, acknowledging the steps taken towards personal development. Rather than focus solely on the results or accomplishments, focus on the journey. Embrace the multifaceted nature of self-expression, allowing yourself the freedom to explore different avenues of creativity and self-discovery. Remember that external achievements do not solely determine self-worth but are deeply rooted in the ongoing process of self-awareness and growth. Approach each day with an open heart and mind, remaining mindful of your progress, no matter how small. By nurturing a positive and supportive mindset, you can cultivate a greater sense of self-esteem and fulfilment in your journey towards personal growth and self-expression.

Grant Yourself Grace Along the Journey

Since childhood, we've been repeatedly reminded that "nobody is perfect" and that "mistakes are a part of life." However, as we age, the pressure to avoid failure can intensify. It is vital to permit yourself to ease up! Embrace mistakes as opportunities for growth and accept your past experiences without judgment. Personal growth is a continuous transformation journey, and imperfection is a natural process. Rather than striving for perfection, embrace the inevitability of making mistakes. Each error offers valuable lessons and insights contributing to your development and understanding. So, don't succumb to the internal pressure to be flawless. Instead, embrace the learning that comes from many mistakes; the wisdom gained will prove invaluable in your journey of self-discovery and growth.

Leave perfectionism behind

People often find themselves overly critical of themselves because they strive for perfection in every aspect of their lives. I held myself to unattainable standards, both academically and in various other elements. However, this mindset came with significant drawbacks, as I often avoided taking action out of fear of not meeting these impossible standards. Sometimes, I convinced myself that specific tasks were too daunting and not worth pursuing, leading me to give up before starting. Recognising the negative impact of this mindset on myself and those around me was the catalyst for change. It prompted me to shift towards a more positive and forgiving outlook, letting go of the need for perfection and embracing a mindset focused on growth and progress.

Putting self-love into practice

When faced with uncomfortable situations, our natural inclination is often to avoid them altogether. For instance, you might think, "Once I've tended to my family's needs, I'll carve out time to focus on my emotions and start journaling." However, this can seem overwhelming and daunting. Instead, start small by identifying one self-care activity you can do today, whether offering yourself words of reassurance or performing a small act of kindness. To further solidify your commitment to self-care, consider creating a list of self-loving actions and specific timelines for accomplishing them. Putting your intentions down on paper enhances accountability and increases the likelihood of follow-through. As you integrate more self-compassionate practices into your daily routine, you will gradually notice a shift in your mindset, reducing self-defeating beliefs and behaviours. Over time, self-love will become second nature through consistent practice.

It is important to understand that self-love isn't about vanity or superiority over others. Instead, it is about recognising and appreciating your inherent worth. When you cultivate self-love, you radiate confidence and attract positivity into your life. To deepen your self-love journey, try viewing yourself through the lens of someone who sees your actual value, free from insecurities and self-doubt. Self-love transcends gender boundaries, as everyone deserves to experience inner happiness and fulfilment. Embracing self-love allows for profound self-reflection, leading to transformative changes in one's life. It is crucial to love and accept ourselves unconditionally, even on our most challenging days. By fostering a healthy self-awareness, we become less reliant on external validation and more focused on our happiness and well-being. Let's never lose sight of the importance of prioritising our self-care and happiness.

6. Self-Love: Won, Not Bought!

"If you have the ability to love, love yourself first."
—Charles Bukowski

I recall a day when I reached out to a friend for assistance with grocery shopping, as I had other pressing matters to attend to. Upon their return, I felt immense gratitude towards my friend for their help. It struck me that my friend could assist me because it was within their capability. Consider asking them to use the restroom on my behalf when in dire need – an impossible request, right? There are specific tasks that others can do for us, while others require our attention. Self-love exemplifies a task that only we can fulfil. No one else can love us the way we can, except for a higher power like God. It is not someone else's responsibility to love us. I've observed many individuals longing for love from others without first cultivating self-love. I firmly believe no one else can love us if we don't love ourselves. Expecting someone else's love when we haven't embraced self-love is akin to asking someone to eat on our behalf and then hoping to feel satiated. It is simply not feasible. Loving ourselves is imperative; in reality, we shouldn't expect others to love us if we don't love ourselves.

Self-love is earned, not acquired. It doesn't come from external sources but rather from within. We must consciously choose to prioritise self-love over the opinions and expectations of others – be it friends, family, or society. We should strive to reflect our authentic selves and not allow external influences to dictate our sense of worth. Unfortunately, many individuals harbour self-hatred due to societal standards regarding appearance or other uncontrollable factors. Instead of dwelling on perceived flaws, why not overcome obstacles and embrace self-love? Entrusting our happiness to others is futile; we must take ownership and prioritise our well-being. We shouldn't settle for anything less than the best, irrespective of others' opinions. This isn't about selfishness, but self-care and prioritising our happiness. Practising self-love isn't as daunting as it may seem; it simply involves living life on our terms. In the following discussion, I'll share practical tips and strategies to help you cultivate self-love without complications.

Avoid comparison

In our competitive society, it is common for individuals to compare themselves. However, this habit can be detrimental. Why compare yourself to someone else when, last I checked, you were the unique individual on this planet? Everyone is inherently different and possesses their qualities and attributes. Therefore, comparing yourself to others serves no purpose. Such comparisons often lead to feelings of inadequacy and self-doubt, as you may perceive yourself as lacking compared to others. Why not focus on self-improvement rather than getting caught up in competition and comparison? Instead of measuring yourself against external standards, strive to become a better version of yourself each day. Challenge yourself to exceed your expectations and track your progress over time. By comparing yourself to who you were yesterday, you will appreciate the growth you have achieved and gain insight into areas for further development.

Don't bother about people's opinions

Disregard the opinions others hold of you; their viewpoints hold no significance. Overthinking their judgments will only drain you. Pay no mind to societal expectations; if they dictate being married by 30, and you're not, let it not trouble you. Your life is not subject to others' directives. Guard your happiness against external pressures. Attempting to satisfy everyone is fruitless. Embracing others' opinions might hinder your self-improvement journey.

Mistakes are unavoidable

"To err is human" is a widely known adage many overlook. Making mistakes is part of being human, so there's no need to beat yourself up over them. Remember your childhood, when your mother would remind you that "nobody is perfect" whenever you made a mistake and couldn't stop crying? That sentiment remains just as accurate today. As you mature, society often portrays mistakes as unforgivable, but they're essential for growth. Without mistakes, you wouldn't learn how to improve. Understand that you're a continual work in progress, evolving each day. So, when you stumble and feel like you have hit rock bottom, refuse to stay down. Instead, gather yourself, brush off the dust, and continue your journey. Let nothing, not even your mistakes, hinder your progress.

You are more than your physical appearance

Your physical appearance doesn't define you. You are more than that short lady everyone sees; you are more than you think; your true self is in you. Society has a way of defining us by gender, height, race, size and many things that don't count. You are valuable, beautiful, awesome and unique, regardless of physical appearance. Whenever you look in the mirror, do not just look at your face; picture the giant in you. Don't be compelled to look or dress like everybody to gain acceptance. Wear what you can afford and make you feel comfortable. When choosing apparel for yourself, whether a designer or not, choose what makes you happy and confident.

Cut off toxic people

Not everyone is meant to be a part of your journey. Some individuals don't add value to your life; they bring negativity and unwanted vibes. During my time dating an ex-boyfriend, I gradually witnessed his toxic, jealous, and overwhelmingly insecure nature. One notable incident occurred during a movie outing when he fell asleep. Not wanting to disturb him, I assumed he was tired from work. However, upon waking up, he accused me of conversing with other men while he slept, implying infidelity. Another instance arose when he unexpectedly requested my phone to make an online purchase despite having a fully functional device. Claiming my phone was faster, a blatant falsehood considering its outdated version, I began to realise the depth of his manipulative behaviour. These encounters served as eye-openers to the toxicity infiltrating our relationship, manifesting in my transformation into a person unrecognisable to myself—marked by heightened anger, bitterness, and irritability. Recognising his detrimental influence, I understood the urgency of severing ties before further harm befell my well-being.

It is crucial to sever ties with such toxic people. Their presence only serves to deplete your energy and foster a hostile atmosphere. Don't hesitate to bid farewell to those who spread negativity; do so without apology. While it may be difficult, prioritising self-love necessitates distancing yourself from energy-draining individuals. By letting go of such connections, you're ultimately benefiting your well-being.

Be mindful

Practising mindfulness involves being fully present in the current moment. It entails diverting your attention from the past and future, focusing solely on the present. While recognising the importance of planning for the future, embracing and appreciating each passing moment is crucial. Overthinking what lies ahead may obstruct your ability to savour the present joy. Engaging in activities like meditation or deep breathing can help centre your mind, enabling you to dispel distractions and fully immerse yourself in the present moment.

Picture yourself seated by a serene lakeside, the stillness of the water reflecting the vibrant hues of the setting sun. As you close your eyes, a gentle breeze whispers through the trees, carrying with it the fragrance of wildflowers. In this tranquil moment, you allow yourself to fully immerse in the present, releasing the weight of past burdens and the anxiety of tomorrow's uncertainties. With each mindful breath, you become attuned to the rhythm of nature—the soft lapping of waves against the shore, the symphony of crickets serenading the evening. You feel a profound connection to the universe, sensing the interconnectedness of all living beings. In this depth of mindfulness, you are not merely a passive observer but an active participant in the unfolding tapestry of life. Your awareness expands beyond the confines of your existence, embracing the vastness of reality itself. In this sacred space of presence, you discover that true peace and fulfilment reside not in the distant past or uncertain future but in the eternal now. And as you surrender to the beauty and wonder of the present moment, you find solace, strength, and an abiding sense of belonging in the vast cosmos.

Be bold

Embrace the courage to voice your thoughts, particularly in public settings. Cultivate the habit of advocating for yourself; refrain from remaining silent when decisions impacting you are under discussion. In group gatherings, resist the urge to merely observe passively; instead, actively engage in conversations, expressing your viewpoints on relevant topics. Recognise the significance of your voice; your input on pertinent matters could offer the breakthrough solution sought by others. Adopt a proactive stance and assertively contribute. Remember, your perspective holds equal weight to that of others present.

Challenge every negative thought

Sometimes, negative thoughts may arise, burdening your mind with doubts such as "I'm worthless, no one appreciates me," or "I'm destined to fail." It is crucial to interrogate and challenge these thoughts when they surface. Instead of succumbing to feelings of failure, inquire into the reasons behind such beliefs. Ask yourself empowering questions like "What actions can lead to success?" or "How can I overcome obstacles?" Redirecting your focus in this manner empowers you to rise above negativity rather than succumb to it. Resist internalising pessimistic thoughts; confront them head-on and promptly discard them.

Additionally, consider how external influences shape your self-perception. For instance, failing to meet others' unrealistic expectations may erroneously lead you to believe you have failed. Recognise that unreasonable expectations are not a reflection of your worth. Moreover, refrain from equating your worth with meeting every demand, especially when the request lacks sincerity. Challenge negative self-assessments by exploring their origins and implementing necessary adjustments. Refuse to let pessimism rule your thoughts; instead, cultivate a mindset grounded in positivity and self-assurance.

Treat yourself kindly

In a world where bitterness often pervades interactions, you need not contribute to the negativity. Despite encountering harsh criticism and destructive remarks from others, resist the temptation to reciprocate in kind. Instead, choose to extend kindness and compassion towards yourself. When faced with negativity from others, counter it by speaking positively about yourself. Offer yourself words of encouragement and affirmation, and consistently acknowledge your worth. Embrace the practice of self-celebration, recognising and honouring your unique qualities and achievements.

Practice self-care

When discussing self-love, it is vital to prioritise self-care. Whether it is nurturing your mental or physical well-being, safeguarding your health is paramount. Indulge in nourishing meals, carve out moments for relaxation, and explore enjoyable activities like visiting cinemas or other stimulating venues. The avenues for self-care are diverse and abundant, so take the time to discover what works best for you. Engage in hiking, hitting the gym, honing your hobbies, or exploring new interests to enhance your overall well-being.

Seek help

Research has indeed demonstrated the effectiveness of therapists in helping individuals cultivate self-love. Therapists play a crucial role in helping individuals understand and address their fears, worries, and anxieties, offering valuable techniques to overcome them. By seeking guidance from a therapist, individuals become more accountable in their journey toward self-love. Therapists monitor progress closely, providing support and encouragement along the way. Instead of attempting to navigate the process alone, it is beneficial to enlist the expertise of professionals who can assist in achieving the goal of loving oneself.

Keep journals

Keeping journals is a powerful tool for self-awareness in our modern world. By jotting down your daily activities, you gain insight into your habits, accomplishments, and areas for improvement. Reflecting on your experiences allows you to identify mistakes, celebrate achievements, and track progress toward your goals. With a journal, you can strategise more effectively, pinpointing the steps needed to succeed. Moreover, journaling helps you discern between productive and unproductive activities, enabling you to optimise your time and focus on what truly matters. Embracing this practice fosters continuous personal growth and empowers you to lead a more intentional and fulfilling life.

Maximise every opportunity

There may never be an ideal moment to take that significant leap forward. However, the crucial thing is to initiate action. Waiting for the perfect timing can lead to missed opportunities, as chances may not repeat themselves. Despite imperfect circumstances, don't let them hinder you from pursuing your dreams. Time is precious and fleeting, and dwelling on missed opportunities can be regretful. Seize every chance that presents itself, for you may not get another. Embracing this mindset ensures that when you finally take that bold step, you will be grateful for having seized the moment.

In closing, let us unravel the profound essence of self-love—it is not just a concept but the cornerstone of your existence. It is the resounding affirmation that you are deserving, worthy, and capable of embracing boundless happiness and success on your terms. Let us acknowledge the formidable journey it entails and its significance. Self-love beckons us to confront our most profound insecurities to challenge the whispers of doubt that echo within. It demands that we wield our inner strength to defy the shadows of self-doubt and rise, resplendent in our authenticity. So, I dare you to embark on this transformative odyssey—to cast aside the shackles of self-critique and embrace the radiant truth of your worthiness. Reject the notion that your value is contingent upon external validation, for within you lies an unfathomable reservoir of strength and beauty waiting to be unleashed. As you traverse this path, remember self-love is not a destination but a profound evolution—a metamorphosis of the soul. It is a symphony of self-compassion, a celebration of your inherent worth, reverberating through every fibre of your being.

So, proclaim it boldly: "I can do it, I will do it." Let these words be the anthem of your self-love journey, guiding you toward a life imbued with fulfilment and joy. Embrace your worth, cherish your uniqueness, and watch in awe as self-love weaves its magic, transforming your world into a tapestry of wonder and possibility. You are worthy. You are enough.

7. Embracing Empathy

"Empathy is a special way of coming to know another and yourself."
—Carl Rogers

Humans are fundamentally distinct entities, each experiencing life as an individual from birth. However, we also integrate into various communities and institutions, from work and education to religious centres and local neighbourhoods. Within these groups, we interact with multiple individuals of different ages, temperaments, and intellects. Participation in these social contexts necessitates cultivating interpersonal skills, with empathy standing out as a crucial component.

What is Empathy?

Empathy transcends mere recognition of emotions; it is the profound ability to delve into the intricacies of others' feelings, understanding their feelings and why they feel that way. It involves stepping into their shoes, viewing the world through their lens, and envisaging oneself in their circumstances. This heightened awareness of others' emotions is a vital bridge between self and society, a cornerstone of emotional intelligence. Beyond mere sympathy, empathy demands a creative leap, a capacity to comprehend the nuances of another's emotional landscape. It entails acknowledging their concerns and grasping the deeper roots of their reactions and sentiments. Empathy is not a universal attribute; its manifestation varies among individuals. While some instinctively empathise with others' distress, others may exhibit apathy or hostility. Such disparities underscore the complex interplay of nature and nurture in shaping our empathetic responses. While empathy fosters genuine concern for others' well-being, it also carries the risk of emotional exhaustion, particularly in those constantly attuned to others' emotional states. The empathetic journey, though rewarding, can be fraught with challenges, leading to burnout and overwhelm. Nevertheless, empathy is not an immutable trait; instead, it is a skill that can be cultivated and honed over time. Like any interpersonal skill, it requires dedication and practice, offering the promise of deeper human connection and understanding.

Empathy manifests through various distinct characteristics, defining those who possess it. These traits encompass:

- Proficiency in active listening, demonstrating a genuine interest in others' narratives.
- People gravitate towards empaths, confiding in them with their struggles and dilemmas.

- An innate ability to intuitively decipher the emotions of others, often without explicit verbal cues.

- Vulnerability to feeling overwhelmed, particularly in the face of tragic or distressing events.

- Difficulty in establishing and maintaining boundaries within interpersonal relationships, leading to potential emotional strain.

- Aptitude for offering insightful advice and guidance, drawing from their deep understanding of human emotions.

- A need for ample solitary time to recharge and recalibrate amidst the emotional demands of empathic engagement.

- Susceptibility to being drained by 'energy vampires,' individuals who exhaust empaths emotionally and energetically.

- Tendency towards introversion, seeking solace and introspection in quieter, more secluded settings.

Empathy encompasses several fundamental components:

Understanding Others: Empathy begins with a genuine interest in comprehending the concerns, emotions, and perspectives of others. Those who understand others actively engage with emotional signals, interpret non-verbal cues adeptly and demonstrate attentive listening skills. Their assistance to others is grounded in a deep understanding of their feelings and experiences.

Developing Others: Empathetic individuals are committed to fostering the growth and potential of those around them. This involves recognising and celebrating others' achievements and offering constructive feedback to enhance their skills and capabilities. Additionally, it encompasses mentorship and coaching, guiding others towards self-improvement and success.

Service Inclination: Empaths view their roles as opportunities for service and support. They prioritise customer satisfaction, consistently seeking ways to exceed expectations and address customer needs. Going above and beyond, they cultivate strong customer relationships, earning their trust and loyalty. In the workplace, empathetic individuals often emerge as trusted advisors, valued for their genuine care and dedication to serving others.

Empathy encompasses various forms:

Affective Empathy involves recognising and responding to the emotions of others, often leading to feelings of concern or personal distress, particularly in intense situations.

Somatic Empathy: In some cases, empathy elicits physical reactions mirroring those of the observed individuals. These responses, such as blushing, facial expressions, or stomach discomfort, signify a physiological resonance with others' experiences.

Cognitive Empathy: Unlike affective empathy, cognitive empathy involves understanding the mental states and thought processes of others in response to a given situation. It functions rationally rather than emotionally and is closely associated with psychology's 'theory of mind' concept.

Humanity's capacity for cruelty and atrocity often surfaces in the headlines of newspapers and news broadcasts. This raises an important question: Why do people engage in harmful behaviours instead of showing empathy in their interactions? What motivates our capacity to empathise, to recognise the pain of others, and to respond with kindness and genuine concern? Practising empathy offers numerous invaluable benefits. Firstly, it fosters meaningful relational bonds between individuals, profoundly enriching our connections with others. Furthermore, empathy equips us to navigate social situations adeptly, guiding our responses in a considerate and appropriate manner. Empathy is pivotal in maintaining psychological well-being, providing a foundation for emotional resilience and stability. By engaging in empathetic understanding, we also cultivate the capacity to regulate our emotions effectively, enhancing our overall emotional intelligence.

Lastly, empathy catalyses altruistic behaviour, inspiring acts of kindness and assistance toward others and fostering a culture of compassion and mutual support within society. Empathy isn't uniformly expressed in every circumstance; it varies among individuals and is shaped by a myriad of factors. Some naturally lean towards empathy more readily than others, and the receptiveness of the recipient can influence this predisposition. Several elements contribute to this inclination.

Firstly, individuals' perceptions of the other party play a significant role, influencing their capacity for empathy based on their understanding of the situation. Secondly, the underlying reasons behind a person's predicament can sway one's empathetic response, with different motivations eliciting varied degrees of empathy. Moreover, past experiences and personal expectations shape one's empathetic tendencies, as individuals draw from their encounters to inform their reactions. Furthermore, research highlights gender disparities in empathy, with women often exhibiting more excellent proficiency in empathy tests and displaying heightened cognitive empathy compared to men. While the findings remain inconclusive, these differences underscore the complex interplay between biology and socialisation in shaping empathetic tendencies.

Ultimately, empathy is deeply rooted in the age-old interplay of nature and nurture. Genetic inheritance contributes to individuals' overall personality traits, while socialisation factors such as familial upbringing, peer interactions, and community influence further mould one's empathetic disposition. Thus, how individuals perceive and respond to others is intricately intertwined with their early upbringing, reflecting the beliefs and values instilled in them from a young age by their social environment.

Numerous barriers obstruct the path to empathy, hindering individuals from embracing and demonstrating this essential virtue in their interactions with others. Here are a few notable barriers:

Cognitive Biases: These biases skew individuals' perceptions of the world, leading them to hastily attribute others' failures to personal flaws while conveniently attributing their shortcomings to external circumstances. Such biases impede individuals from recognising the multifaceted nature of situations and hinder their ability to empathise by preventing them from adopting others' perspectives.

Dehumanisation: When individuals perceive others as fundamentally different or distant from themselves, they struggle to empathise with their experiences. This phenomenon is particularly evident in instances such as natural disasters or conflicts in distant regions, where unaffected individuals fail to empathise with the suffering of others due to a perceived sense of separation or disconnection.

Victim Blaming: When individuals endure unfortunate or traumatic experiences, there is a regrettable tendency for some to shift blame onto the victim, questioning their actions or suggesting they could have avoided their predicament. This inclination stems from the misguided belief in a just and fair world, where individuals supposedly reap what they sow. However, this belief overlooks the unpredictable nature of life and the myriad external factors beyond individuals' control that can influence their circumstances.

These barriers to empathy highlight the complex interplay of cognitive biases, social perceptions, and societal norms that impede individuals from extending compassion and understanding towards others in times of need. Overcoming these barriers requires a concerted effort to challenge ingrained biases, cultivate empathy, and foster a deeper appreciation for the shared humanity that unites us all.

Connection is an innate human requirement, fostering trust, security, and acceptance within our relationships with others and ourselves. Empathy is the conduit for such connections, allowing us to understand and relate to others without prejudice or fear. We can transcend negative emotions like anger, loneliness, and distrust by embracing empathy. Here are three pivotal steps to cultivate empathy:

Assume Positive Intentions: Reframe your perspective to assume positive intentions behind these actions, rather than react angrily to undesirable behaviour. This shift in mindset fosters empathy and understanding, paving the way for deeper connections.

Recognise the Root Cause: Behaviour is often the final manifestation of a complex interplay of internal and external factors. By recognising that actions stem from unmet needs or emotions, we can approach situations with empathy and compassion rather than judgment.

Prioritise Curiosity Over Judgment: Instead of hastily passing judgment on others, cultivate curiosity about the underlying motives driving their behaviour. By seeking to understand rather than to condemn, we open the door to genuine connection and empathy.

By embracing empathy and following these steps, we can foster meaningful connections built on understanding, compassion, and acceptance.

Aspects of life where empathy is essential

In Personal Life: Our journeys are intricately woven with the threads of interpersonal connections. The vitality of these relationships hinges upon our capacity for empathy, whether within the bounds of platonic camaraderie or romantic entanglements. A relationship devoid of empathy resembles a fragile vessel adrift on stormy seas, destined to founder upon the rocks of misunderstanding. Consider, for instance, a marriage where one partner fails to empathise with the other's perspective—the seeds of discord are sown, and the union teeters on the brink of collapse. Given the inherent diversity of human experiences, values, and struggles, it is imperative that both parties in any relationship endeavour to bridge the chasm of understanding, lest they find themselves adrift in a sea of loneliness and neglect.

In Work Life: Within the tapestry of the professional realm, where individuals of varied backgrounds converge, harmonious coexistence is woven through the threads of empathy. Whether colleagues find themselves in the same department or on disparate projects, fostering amicable relations is essential to cultivating an atmosphere of camaraderie, fostering friendships and nurturing a robust team spirit. Furthermore, it is incumbent upon managers and leaders to exhibit empathy towards their subordinates, for leaders devoid of empathy are prone to enforcing Draconian policies and unreasonable demands, fostering an environment of discontent and disengagement. By contrast, empathetic leaders inspire their teams to excel, crafting remuneration packages and benefits that foster loyalty and incentivise wholehearted commitment.

Businesses that embrace empathy in their ethos reap the rewards of increased sales, unwavering loyalty, and effusive word-of-mouth endorsements. By truly understanding the needs of their clientele—listening to their desires, addressing their grievances, and valuing their contributions—enterprises cultivate a legion of devoted advocates. Such a culture of empathy must permeate every facet of the organisation, from frontline customer service to the hallowed halls of the accounting department, for it is through empathy that businesses forge enduring connections with their clientele.

On a Global Scale: When viewed from a global perspective, empathy serves as a guiding light for leaders developing policies that cross national borders. It compels nations to extend a helping hand in times of natural calamities, fostering a sense of solidarity and shared humanity. Moreover, empathy promotes international collaborations to advance global development, as nations recognise that their destinies are intertwined in the fabric of our shared planet. Empathy goes beyond individual differences, fostering collective progress and promoting global harmony.

How to improve your level of empathy

Encouraging empathy in children is often viewed as a more straightforward task, and fostering empathy in adults is not beyond reach. There are several avenues through which adults can enhance their empathetic capacity:

Engaging with Literary Fiction: Delving into the realms of literary fiction can serve as a potent catalyst for empathy growth. Research suggests that when individuals immerse themselves in fictional narratives, they embark on empathetic journeys, traversing diverse landscapes of human experience. Through the eyes of fictional characters, readers gain access to inner worlds and emotions, transcending the boundaries of their own lived experiences. For instance, a reader in the United States may find common ground with characters inhabiting distant African landscapes, illuminating shared humanity amidst cultural differences. By peering into the intimate thoughts and feelings of fictional personas, literature offers a unique vantage point for cultivating empathy, expanding our capacity to understand and relate to others.

Understanding Those with Differing Beliefs: It is natural for individuals to gravitate towards their "in-group," where shared beliefs and values create a sense of familiarity and comfort. However, such insular tendencies can hinder the development of empathy, particularly in environments characterised by diversity. Individuals must actively challenge entrenched biases and broaden their social circles to foster empathy. We confront preconceived notions and expand our empathetic horizons by connecting with individuals from diverse backgrounds. Surprising commonalities may emerge, fostering mutual understanding and deepening our capacity to empathise with different perspectives. Through such encounters, empathy transcends barriers, encouraging a more inclusive and compassionate society.

Embracing empathy as a core lifestyle value would require some self-preservation techniques to prevent people from taking advantage of you. Here are some self-preservation techniques for those who navigate the world with open hearts:

Recognise Your Empathetic Essence: Embracing empathy means embracing the innate inclination to withhold judgment and seek understanding in the tapestry of human emotions. Acknowledging this inherent trait is the first step towards preserving the essence of one's inner light and vitality.

Trust Your Intuition: For empaths, intuition is a guiding compass, finely attuned to the subtle nuances of human interaction. Whether deciphering non-verbal cues or sensing the unspoken thoughts of others, trusting one's intuition is crucial for navigating the delicate dance of relationships and avoiding the pitfalls of negative energy.

Avoid the Victim Mentality: Empaths, in their boundless compassion, often neglect their own needs, risking a descent into the depths of victimhood. By recognising and asserting their worth, empaths reclaim agency over their lives, forging a path of self-empowerment and resilience.

Establish Healthy Boundaries: Identifying individuals who deplete one's energy reserves is vital for maintaining emotional equilibrium. Setting clear boundaries delineates the sacred space where one's well-being takes precedence, shielding against the draining influence of energy vampires.

Cultivate Inner Stillness: In the hustle and bustle of life, empaths require moments of tranquillity to recharge their spirits. They anchor themselves in the present moment through meditation and mindful breathing, releasing pent-up negativity and restoring inner harmony.

Cherish Self-Love: As an empath, it is good to take care of yourself. Consider self-care as crucial as your empathetic actions toward others. Take time to listen to your thoughts and emotions. Recognise that you are strong and vulnerable. Revel in the moments when you listen to your feelings and take action to make yourself happier. Remember that when you live up to your potential, you increase your power to transform the lives of others. By embracing empathy as more than a trait but a way of life, individuals unlock the doors to profound joy and self-fulfilment. Grounded in authenticity and connected to their true essence, empaths radiate a beauty that transcends the superficial, enriching the world with their boundless compassion.

Part Three
Winning The Battle

8. Leaving The Past Behind

"Past can never become your present, but the present can become your future."
—Unknown

There exist moments in life that elevate you to cloud nine, leaving you with an everlasting grin whenever they dance across your memory. Conversely, some episodes weigh heavily on your heart, haunting your thoughts and robbing you of sleep. These instances cling to your conscience, burdening you with guilt and self-condemnation, making it arduous to bid them farewell. Furthermore, the fear of history repeating itself can cast a shadow over the prospect, instilling apprehension in your heart. However, such experiences are universal; nobody traverses life's journey unscathed. Nevertheless, dwelling in the past is not sustainable; it is imperative to forge ahead. Some things are best left in the annals of yesteryears, as clinging onto them often yields more harm than good. Indeed, ruminating over past events seldom yields any positive outcome. If you question why, it is necessary to relinquish the past, fret not, for I shall explain the strategies to facilitate this transition.

You cannot change the past

No matter how much you wish, you can't rewind the clock and undo the past. What's done is done, so there's no reason to dwell on things that cannot be changed. Clinging to the past only drains your energy and prevents you from fully embracing the present and looking forward to the future.

Life is short

Life is too short, so don't let your past tie you down. You know the famous saying, "You only live once." You don't have more than one life, so why should you not live it to the optimum? Why should you live in the bondage of your past when your time is ticking now and then? Before you know it, you will have grey hairs on your head, and you won't have the strength to do what you wish you had done. *"As for man, his days are as grass: As a flower of the field, so he flourisheth. For the wind passeth over it, and it is gone; And the place thereof shall know it no more." Psalm 103: 15-16 KJV.*

You are disrespectful to yourself

Choosing to dwell in the past instead of directing your attention towards the present and future indicates a lack of self-respect and self-worth. Why would you dwell on the past instead of focusing on your well-being, happiness, and aspirations? Frankly, such behaviour disrespects your authentic self; the individual who clings to the past is not a true reflection of who you are.

You should write your story

Choosing to let the past define you is akin to handing over the pen of your life's story to someone or something else. You relinquish control by dwelling on past experiences, allowing them to dictate your identity and shape your narrative. However, if faced with such a predicament, I would seize the pen, flip to a blank page, and commence crafting a new chapter filled with beauty, resilience, and the freedom to chart my own path.

You are limiting yourself

If you choose to hold on to the past, it is like building a wall around yourself. That only means one thing, and it is that you can't move forward. Living in the past is like walking backwards; I am sure you know what that means. You will only stop yourself from reaching your goals and the apex of your life if you curdle your past as if it were a child. So don't hinder yourself; let the past go, and you will be amazed at how far you will run to achieve your goals and dreams.

Many people don't want to hear the bitter truth that it is your choice to leave the past behind. You can choose to hold on to the past and allow it to keep haunting you, or move on to enjoy a life of happiness. It all depends on you. Tony Robbins said something profound, and I should let you know. "Your past does not equal your future unless you choose to live there." The question is, do you want to live there? I don't know your answer, but I want you to know that you cannot have a good life if you choose to live in your past. Your relationship with yourself and others will be affected if you live in your past. You must consider the present and the beautiful future you want to create. When you leave the past behind and pay attention to the present, you will experience happiness and an effective relationship with yourself and others. If you want to leave the past behind and become free from the bond it has put you in, follow the strategies I will discuss below. I am sure they will help you if you use them and intentionally leave your past behind.

Don't deny your past

In the quest to move beyond the past, it is essential to confront and acknowledge what transpired rather than sweep it under the rug. Denying the reality of past events only perpetuates their hold over us. Instead, I advocate for an approach of acceptance, where we acknowledge the occurrences without dwelling on them excessively. By embracing the truth of our past, we allow ourselves to glean valuable lessons from our experiences. Mistakes serve as influential teachers, illuminating the path towards personal growth and development. Every setback presents a chance to refine ourselves, emerging stronger and wiser. When we glean insights from our past, we no longer feel the need to conceal it; instead, we eagerly share the wisdom gained and the strides made towards self-improvement.

Express yourself

Do not hesitate to release the burden; seek avenues to unburden your mind. Initiating a dialogue with the individual who inflicted harm upon you or whom you have wronged can be cathartic. Alternatively, confiding in a trusted friend or even jotting down your thoughts can provide solace. When you articulate your emotions, letting go becomes more attainable, consigning the past to its rightful place. Moreover, expressing oneself is crucial for mental well-being. Medical experts have underscored the detrimental effects of bottling up emotions, including depression, hypertension, anxiety, and headaches. Confiding in a sympathetic listener can be invaluable in overcoming the past. Sharing your feelings allows you to articulate your pain, facilitating the process of release and healing.

Stop blaming others

It can be tempting to assume the role of the victim when confronted with adversity, as it offers temporary solace and absolves one from accepting responsibility. However, assigning blame to others for past misfortunes only impedes personal growth and hinders progress. Engaging in a cycle of complaint and finger-pointing relinquishes one's agency, granting power to external forces. Essentially, one surrenders their autonomy by laying blame elsewhere, diminishing their stature. Blaming others fosters a negative mindset and signifies an unwillingness to take ownership of one's life. Instead of moving forward, this behaviour perpetuates a cycle of stagnation and resentment.

Live in the present

Embracing the present moment is a potent antidote to the lingering grip of the past. Instead of being trapped in the echoes of the past, we can actively engage in the abundance of the present moment. Engaging in myriad activities can help divert our attention from past grievances and infuse our lives with vitality and joy. Whether meditation, embracing a writing challenge, participating in contests, acquiring new skills, attending dance classes, socialising with friends, volunteering, or exploring nature through hiking, the key is finding activities that ignite our passion and capture our focus. By immersing ourselves in pursuits that exhilarate and invigorate, we enhance our capacity to bid farewell to the past and forge ahead.

Living in the moment necessitates mindfulness—a state wherein we are attuned to our thoughts and emotions. Psychologists affirm that individuals who cultivate mindfulness exhibit more excellent emotional stability, compassion, and happiness. To cultivate mindfulness, we must acknowledge our thoughts and feelings without judgment. Rather than magnifying trivial issues into insurmountable obstacles, we can accept negative emotions as natural facets of human experience. Moreover, actively seeking out novel experiences fosters mindfulness and enriches our lives. Instead of dwelling on past grievances, let us embrace the present moment with open arms, fostering a sense of gratitude and contentment in our daily lives.

Get guidance

When breaking free from the shackles of the past becomes insurmountable, seeking professional guidance is a wise step forward. Professionals possess a wealth of expertise that can facilitate your journey toward letting go of the past. With their extensive experience in assisting clients grappling with similar challenges, they offer invaluable insights and strategies for overcoming past traumas and moving forward unencumbered. Seeking professional assistance is not a sign of weakness, as some may perceive; it underscores one's inner strength and resilience. It signifies a willingness to confront and conquer personal obstacles, demonstrating a commendable commitment to self-improvement and emotional well-being.

Disengage for a moment

Grant yourself the gift of respite to clear your mind and regain perspective. Taking a step back doesn't necessarily entail embarking on an elaborate journey spanning a continent; it simply involves disengaging from environments, individuals, or objects that serve as constant reminders of the past. Distancing oneself from such triggers opens the door to exploring new and uplifting experiences. Whether it is reconnecting with family, visiting a friend in a different town, or temporarily disconnecting from social media, the aim is to create space for positive engagement. Upon returning, your outlook on the past transforms, allowing for renewed clarity and a refreshed perspective.

Stop being negative

When confronted with adversity, it is essential to recognise that it does not signify the culmination of your life's journey. Often, the weight of a negative experience can feel overwhelming, leading to self-destructive thoughts such as believing that misfortune is your only companion or that the world is against you. However, clinging to these notions serves only to tether you to the past, preventing yesterday's wounds from healing and perpetuating a cycle of pain. Within the shadows is an indomitable light—the unwavering resilience within you. Regardless of the trials you have faced, you possess the innate capacity to rise above, to stand tall once more, and to forge ahead with unwavering determination. It is a testament to the human spirit's boundless strength and steadfast resolve.

Instead of succumbing to the shackles of negativity, dare to challenge each pessimistic thought with the power of positivity. Affirmations such as "I am capable of overcoming any obstacle," "My future brims with boundless potential," and "I refuse to be defined by the shadows of my past" can serve as guiding beacons, illuminating the path toward a brighter tomorrow. Embrace the transformative power of positive thinking, and let it permeate every facet of your being. You reclaim agency over your narrative and pave the way for a future imbued with hope, resilience, and unyielding optimism.

Consider your association

Be discerning about the company you choose to surround yourself with, as they can significantly influence your mindset and trajectory in life. Look closely at those within your social circle and identify those who consistently emit negativity or sow seeds of doubt about your abilities. Similarly, recognise those closely associated with the past you're striving to leave behind, as their presence may inadvertently tether you to old patterns and hinder your progress. To break free from the constraints of the past and begin a journey toward a brighter future, it is essential to distance yourself from those who maintain a mindset of stagnation. Doing so allows you to forge new connections with individuals who champion growth, resilience, and forward momentum. Embrace the opportunity to expand your social horizons by actively seeking like-minded individuals who share your aspirations and values. Whether it is through attending conferences, cultural events or simply spending time in places where people gather, be proactive in cultivating relationships that nurture your personal and professional development.

Remember, the path to personal transformation often begins with the company we keep. Surround yourself with individuals who uplift, inspire, and challenge you to become the best version of yourself. In doing so, you will create a supportive network of allies who will bolster your efforts to leave the past behind and embrace the boundless potential of the future.

Forgiveness is key

Forgiveness becomes paramount when aiming to break free from the clutches of the past. It is the key that unlocks the chains binding you to haunting memories. Forgiveness isn't solely about absolving others of their transgressions; it extends to granting yourself the same grace. Holding on to bitterness towards yourself or others only prolongs your stay in the prison of the past. The adage goes, "To forgive is to set a prisoner free and discover that the prisoner was you." Refusing to forgive someone who has wronged you only inflicts further harm upon yourself. Holding on to grudges is akin to self-inflicted wounds, a futile act of self-sabotage.

While relinquishing the past's grip, it is crucial to understand that fallibility is inherent to the human condition. We all stumble and inadvertently cause harm to others. Rather than berating yourself for past mistakes or nursing animosity towards those who have wronged you, seize the opportunity to glean wisdom from these experiences and embark on a path of self-improvement.

True liberation from the past is achieved when you relinquish anger, bitterness, and resentment. By cultivating a spirit of forgiveness towards others and yourself, you pave the way for healing, growth, and a brighter future unencumbered by the shadows of the past.

Create new memories

Leaving the past behind requires deliberate intentionality. You must actively strive to cultivate new, joyful memories that overshadow the negative ones from your past. Invest your time creating beautiful moments with loved ones, engaging in activities that bring you genuine happiness, and seeking solace in places that rejuvenate your spirit. These intentional efforts to forge new memories serve as a powerful antidote to the grip of the past. Research indicates that overcoming the past becomes more challenging when inundated with many old memories. Therefore, the path to liberation necessitates the creation of fresh, positive experiences to supplant the old ones.

In conclusion, the past harbours numerous elements capable of stifling personal growth and eroding self-esteem, making it imperative to release its hold. By applying the wisdom acquired from past experiences, albeit through concerted effort and dedication, you can gradually disentangle yourself from its grasp. Understand that this journey is not instantaneous; it demands time, perseverance, and unwavering resolve. Know that within you lies the power to emancipate yourself from the past's shackles and embrace a new beginning. As you bid farewell to the burdens of yesterday, anticipate improvements in various facets of your life—enhanced relationships, bolstered self-confidence, and the attainment of remarkable accomplishments. While the endeavour to leave the past behind may pose challenges, remember that it is possible and within your reach. Upon emancipation from the past's bondage, a life adorned with happiness and tranquillity awaits you—a life you truly deserve. Remind yourself that the past is immutable. However, you possess the agency to transcend its influence and relinquish its hold over your present and future.

Here's to embracing a fresh start—a journey filled with boundless possibilities and newfound freedom. Cheers to your resilience and the promise of a brighter tomorrow!

9. Mindset and Personal Growth

"Every experience, whether positive or negative, contributes to my growth."
—Unknown

Your mindset wields unparalleled influence over the trajectory of your life, permeating every aspect with its subtle and profound effects. Nurturing a positive mindset emerges as an indispensable cornerstone in the pursuit of personal fulfilment and holistic well-being. By imbuing your outlook with optimism, you unlock the door to many benefits that ripple throughout your existence. When you focus on the positive aspects of life, you liberate yourself from the shackles of past regrets and anxieties about the future. Instead, you anchor yourself firmly in the present moment, where gratitude blossoms and the abundance of the world unfolds before your eyes. In embracing the notion that the glass is half full, you invite a sense of appreciation and contentment to permeate your daily experiences. It is crucial to understand that cultivating a positive mindset doesn't mean denying life's inevitable challenges. Instead, it involves confronting adversity with a resilience forged in the crucible of optimism. Adopting a growth mindset empowers you to view obstacles as opportunities for growth and transformation, fuelling your journey with hope and determination.

At the heart of cultivating a positive mindset lies mindful self-talk—a dialogue that reverberates throughout your consciousness, shaping your perceptions and beliefs. By cultivating an awareness of your inner narrative, you gain insight into whether your thoughts are catalysts for growth or barriers to progress. Recognising that the quality of your thoughts directly influences your outlook underscores the importance of fostering positivity within.

Indeed, the prevailing tone of your inner dialogue serves as a barometer of your overall mindset. If negativity pervades your thoughts, you're more susceptible to adopting a pessimistic worldview. Conversely, a predominance of positive self-talk signals an inclination towards optimism and a belief in the transformative power of positive thinking. In essence, the journey towards a positive mindset is one of profound transformation—a journey that begins with introspection and unfolds through intentional efforts to nurture optimism and resilience. By harnessing the inherent potential for growth within, you pave the way for a life suffused with joy, fulfilment, and boundless possibilities.

What is a fixed mindset?

A fixed mindset constrains one's perception of knowledge and skills, operating under the belief that these attributes are predetermined. Those adhering to such a mindset perceive success as contingent upon innate abilities rather than effort or growth. Essentially, they view themselves as possessing or lacking the inherent qualities necessary for excellence in a given endeavour. A prime illustration of the detrimental effects of a fixed mindset can be gleaned from the case of Nokia, a once-dominant player in the mobile phone industry. Despite its stature, Nokia's failure to adapt its operating system to a more advanced platform is a poignant example of fixed thinking in action. The company's reluctance to embrace change, driven by a fear of competition from rival brands like Samsung, ultimately proved to be its undoing.

By clinging steadfastly to outdated practices and refusing to innovate, Nokia fell victim to the pitfalls of a fixed mindset. In failing to recognise the potential for growth and adaptation, the company squandered opportunities for advancement and ultimately suffered a significant setback in the fiercely competitive smartphone market. The cautionary tale of Nokia serves as a stark reminder of the perils associated with entrenched fixed mindsets; in an ever-evolving landscape where adaptability and innovation reign supreme, success hinges not on static abilities but on a willingness to embrace change and cultivate a growth-oriented mindset.

Buhlebethu S. Mpofu

What is a growth mindset?

A growth mindset embodies a philosophy wherein individuals harbour a steadfast belief in the capacity to amplify their talents, intellect, and capabilities. Those who embrace this mindset perceive themselves as perpetual learners, continuously seeking novel avenues for self-improvement and skill enhancement. When confronted with challenges, individuals wielding a growth mindset refract adversity through the prism of opportunity. Rather than succumbing to defeat, they greet challenges as fertile ground for growth and learning. They eschew notions of failure, recognising that setbacks catalyse personal development and refinement.

Central to the ethos of a growth mindset is the conviction that success is not bestowed by chance or happenstance but rather earned through diligent effort and perseverance. Those who espouse this mindset understand that the pathway to achievement is paved not by luck but by the sweat of one's brow. They acknowledge that each exertion of effort incrementally augments the probability of serendipitous outcomes.

Essentially, a growth mindset transcends mere cognition; it represents a way of life characterised by an insatiable thirst for knowledge and a boundless capacity for self-improvement. By embracing the ethos of growth, individuals unlock the door to a future brimming with possibility and unfettered potential.

Growth mindset versus fixed mindset

Dr Dweck, a respected psychologist, asserts that the contrasting mindsets of fixed and growth originate in early development, profoundly influencing our behaviour, relationships, and responses to success and failure. She elucidates this dichotomy by stating:

"When you harbour the belief that your qualities are immutable, you feel compelled to continually prove your worth. If you perceive your intelligence, personality, and moral character as fixed commodities, you strive to demonstrate proficiency in each, lest you appear deficient in these fundamental attributes."

Unlike the growth mindset, fixed thinking is inherently limiting and can precipitate many challenges throughout one's life. The fear of failure instigates a hyper-focus on areas of perceived strength, dissuading individuals from venturing beyond their comfort zones. Moreover, a fixed worldview impairs the individual harbouring it and casts a pall over their social interactions. Those entrenched in fixed thinking are prone to viewing others as adversaries rather than sources of inspiration. Consequently, they struggle to celebrate the achievements of their peers, impeding the cultivation of meaningful friendships.

Breaking free from the confines of a fixed mindset necessitates a fundamental shift in perspective, whereby one embraces the potential for growth and development. This entails a willingness to confront challenges head-on, embracing failure as a stepping stone rather than a stumbling block. To foster the transition towards a growth mindset, it is imperative to introspect and evaluate one's readiness for change. Are you prepared to relinquish the safety of familiarity in pursuit of personal growth? Are you willing to embrace failure as an inherent aspect of the learning process?

Here are a few actionable steps to facilitate this transformative journey towards a growth mindset:

- Embrace failure as a natural and essential component of growth.

- Cultivate a sense of curiosity and openness to new experiences.

- Develop resilience in the face of setbacks, viewing them as opportunities for learning and growth.

- Surround yourself with individuals who embody the principles of a growth mindset, fostering a supportive environment conducive to personal development.

By adopting these practices and committing to cultivating a growth mindset, you empower yourself to transcend the limitations of fixed thinking and embark on a journey of continuous growth and self-discovery.

Every circumstance should be viewed as a steppingstone

The fear of failure often intertwines with apprehension about the unknown. However, by embracing challenges, analysing setbacks, and cultivating patience, individuals can transform challenges into opportunities for growth and mastery. Experimenting with challenges provides a platform for learning and adaptation. Rather than shying away from complex tasks, approach them with curiosity and a willingness to explore new possibilities. Through experimentation, you gain valuable insights into your strengths and weaknesses, laying the groundwork for future success.

Analysing failures is another crucial aspect of overcoming the fear of failure. Instead of viewing setbacks as insurmountable obstacles, dissect them to uncover valuable lessons. Reflecting on what went wrong and how you can improve fosters resilience and equips you with the knowledge needed to navigate similar challenges in the future. Learning to be patient is essential when facing adversity. Rome wasn't built in a day, nor was mastery achieved overnight. Embrace the journey of growth, understanding that progress takes time and perseverance. Cultivate patience with yourself as you strive to overcome obstacles and achieve your goals. Every time you start over, you take a step closer to mastery. Each attempt, each setback, and each triumph contribute to your growth and development. Embrace the learning and improvement process, knowing that with each new beginning, you inch closer to realising your full potential.

Criticism can be beneficial

Individuals with a fixed mindset often disregard criticism because it can bruise their ego. However, adopting a different perspective and viewing criticism as a valuable asset is crucial. Embracing feedback allows for personal growth and development. Rather than feeling defensive, it is beneficial to approach criticism with an open mind, recognising it as an opportunity to enhance one's skills and abilities. This shift in mentality is essential for fostering a growth mindset.

There is always room for improvement

Enriching your vocabulary with favourable terms and avoiding viewing everything is crucial. Life is complex and offers opportunities for growth and improvement. Acknowledging that perfection is unattainable allows us to embrace our imperfections as opportunities for growth and development. Recognising areas for enhancement doesn't equate to failure; rather, it signifies a willingness to evolve and progress.

Reflect!

We highlighted the significance of embracing mistakes as opportunities for personal growth. If uncertain about the next steps, consider the following approach: dedicate yourself to maintaining a reflective journal. This involves documenting your experiences, conducting self-analysis, and identifying areas for improvement.

What is the relationship between introspection and a growth mindset?

Without reflecting on your experiences, acquiring new knowledge or understanding your mistakes becomes exceedingly difficult. Your reflective notebook serves as a safe space to express your thoughts freely and, notably, preserves them for future review and introspection.

Why a positive mindset matters

Maintaining a cheerful mindset profoundly impacts every facet of life. By embracing positivity, one shifts one's focus from problems to possibilities, setting the stage for success. This optimistic outlook fosters a proactive approach towards the future, enabling the establishment of ambitious goals and the relentless pursuit of their realisation. The influence of positive thinking extends beyond psychological benefits to significant physical and mental well-being enhancements. Individuals who cultivate positivity often experience heightened energy levels, expedited recovery from illnesses, reduced rates of depression, enhanced coping mechanisms, fewer common ailments, and even an elongated lifespan. Moreover, a positive outlook correlates with an overall elevated quality of life, aligning with the universal aspiration for fulfilment and contentment. Acknowledging occasional lapses into negativity is a natural aspect of being human. It is important not to chastise oneself for experiencing fleeting negative thoughts; instead, it is an opportunity for self-compassion and growth.

Negative thoughts, while sometimes inevitable, can serve a purpose in sharpening focus. However, once their utility is fulfilled, it is essential to transform negativity into positivity. A proven five-step strategy exists for this conversion, offering a structured approach towards nurturing a constructive mindset and harnessing the power of optimism for personal growth and wellbeing.

Focus on the present

Refusing to dwell excessively on past mistakes is crucial for personal growth. Instead, staying grounded in the present lets us focus on current actions and opportunities. While feeling regret over past missteps is natural, fixating on them only hinders progress. Acknowledge the lessons learned, let go of the past, and channel efforts into present and future endeavours. This approach fosters resilience and empowers individuals to embrace positive change and pursue their aspirations with renewed vigour.

Find humour in every situation

In many cases, the challenging situations we encounter can be seen in a humorous light. Choosing to respond with laughter can significantly lighten the mood. For instance, if a joke falls flat among friends, instead of dwelling on it negatively, opt to brush it off and carry on with a light-hearted attitude. Ultimately, how we perceive and react to events is within our control. Embracing a positive outlook not only helps to dispel negative emotions but also transforms adverse experiences into opportunities for joy and growth.

Look for the lesson

Negative situations often offer valuable lessons for personal growth and improvement. When faced with adversity, take the opportunity to reflect on the experience and identify what you can learn from it. Perhaps you could have devoted more time to preparation for a tournament or refined your presentation skills. Embracing these moments as opportunities for learning enables you to extract insights even from negative thoughts and experiences.

Reverse the story's narrative

During challenging times, it is essential to acknowledge that there are alternative perspectives to explore. To shift from a negative to a positive outlook, consider reframing the present moment. Is there a silver lining or an opportunity for growth amidst adversity? Embracing a mindset focused on learning and improvement can lead to constructive thinking, such as reflecting on past mistakes and formulating proactive strategies for future actions.

Misconceptions about having a growth mindset

I have it already, and I always have
The misconception often arises when people equate having a growth mindset with inherent traits like adaptability, open-mindedness, or optimism, assuming they've always possessed these qualities. However, this perspective overlooks the reality that individuals possess a combination of fixed and growth mindsets, which evolve with experience. It is essential to recognise that there's no such thing as a "pure" growth mindset, and acknowledging this is essential to fully harnessing the benefits it offers.

Good things happen when you have a growth mentality
Recognising that the path of growth and learning is often complex and unpredictable is essential. Despite efforts, not all endeavours lead to success; just as some gambles may not yield positive outcomes, pursuing innovation can sometimes hit roadblocks.

Anyone can accomplish anything

The growth mindset concept suggests that intelligence and talent are not fixed, but can be developed over time. However, it is important to avoid the misconception that anyone can become anything with enough effort. While hard work is undoubtedly crucial, it is not the sole determinant of success. The reality is that we all have inherent limitations and varying levels of potential. Embracing a growth mindset involves recognising and accepting these limitations while striving to maximise our abilities through dedicated effort and continuous learning.

10. Winning Your Love

"Love wins, love always wins."
—Mitch Albom

In today's world, the pressure to be perfect often overshadows the importance of simply feeling good. When we think of self-love, it might seem as easy as flipping through a self-help book, but it is so much more than that. Our society pushes us to compete, whether with others or even with ourselves, constantly. We always strive to meet deadlines, impress our bosses, and keep up with everyone else's expectations. Many of us feel guilty if we work long hours and don't get enough sleep. Still, we push ourselves to do more and be better. Even when we're supposed to relax or have fun on the weekends, it can feel like we're failing if we're not constantly productive. As a result, we end up being hard on ourselves without even realising it. We spend so much time and energy loving and caring for others—our friends, family, partners, and children—but do we do the same for ourselves? That's the real question. Are we giving ourselves the love and attention we deserve, or always putting others first? "Prioritising our own well-being is equally vital as caring for those around us."

The notion of self-love emerges from recognising that we cannot perpetually rely on external sources for validation and affection. Embracing self-love entails cultivating a sense of empowerment and inner contentment independent of external circumstances. It is about recognising that prioritising oneself isn't selfishness but a fundamental aspect of well-being. In practising self-love, we liberate ourselves from the need for external validation and find fulfilment from within. Acknowledging our humanity and inherent fallibility, we grant ourselves the same compassion and forgiveness we readily extend to our loved ones. It is a process of understanding that making mistakes is intrinsic to our human experience and embracing imperfection as an essential part of our journey. In doing so, we embark on a path of self-acceptance and resilience, allowing ourselves the grace to falter and grow without undue self-criticism.

Embracing self-love and relinquishing negativity is essential for personal growth, as challenges are transient, yielding brighter days ahead. Self-esteem offers manifold advantages. Firstly, nurturing self-love fosters a more optimistic outlook on life. Secondly, it motivates the cultivation of positive habits. Loving oneself encompasses valuing every facet of one's body, spirit, and mind, shielding against external attempts to diminish self-worth. Consequently, self-love promotes a conscientious avoidance of behaviours detrimental to one's well-being. Recognising low self-esteem often manifests through self-doubt, harsh self-criticism, and a persistent sense of inadequacy.

Signs that you don't love yourself adequately

Our disconnection from love is at the heart of almost all our problems. It can lead to a life of mundane desperation—trapping ourselves in boring everyday life or boring relationships, needing love, caring for others at our own expense, or limiting ourselves to what we think we get or what others allow us to do. Low self-esteem often comes from thinking, "I don't deserve to be loved." It is an unrealistic fear – but if you're too afraid to explore it, you won't know. When you lack self-love, you start looking for love outside of yourself, hoping to find someone who will accept you the way you are. After all, the truth is that the only person who can change that belief is yourself. Self-love is about admiring and enjoying your personality. Self-love comes when you decide to study yourself and understand who you are. Loving yourself involves doing many things. It consists in treating yourself with kindness, being devoted to yourself, and taking good care of yourself. It also means accepting who you are – self-acceptance is crucial to self-love. Can you honestly say that you are all these things to yourself? If you can't, you might have difficulty finding true happiness.

Here are four self-degrading signs that you lack self-love:

Excessive Neediness

Seeking excessive attention and acceptance from others often leads to being perceived as overly emotional, which can inadvertently push people away. This behaviour stems from a deep-seated need for validation, but strains relationships when it becomes too demanding.

Strained Family Dynamics

A problematic relationship with relatives can arise from being self-centred, oversensitive, and self-righteous. This defensive stance impedes healthy communication and fosters misunderstandings, hindering the development of meaningful connections.

Unhealthy Eating Habits

Struggling with a bad eating habit, characterised by denying hunger and excessive exercise, often stems from an intense fear of gaining weight and a negative body image. This unhealthy relationship with food reflects an underlying lack of self-love and acceptance.

Constant Vigilance

Feeling abnormally alert and constantly seeking approval and validation in social interactions indicates a deep-seated insecurity and fear of making mistakes. This hypervigilance stifles authenticity, preventing one's true self from shining through and hindering genuine connections with others.

Benefits of self-love

When you love everything about yourself, life reflects that back to you. Loving yourself is crucial to your success in life. When you learn to love yourself completely, you create a happy, conducive environment to thrive in. When we forget the essential thing—self-love—we forget our goals and dreams of being happy and healthy. After all, to live a fulfilling life, you must love everything you have and believe that life will love you. Love is the foundation of who you were born to be. Therefore, training yourself to love daily is crucial to bring you real and lasting happiness and peace of mind and improving your health and well-being. How you talk to yourself is how you feel about yourself, reflecting on your life journey. When you love yourself more, do it with gratitude.

When you embrace self-love wholeheartedly, you cultivate a positive outlook that resonates throughout your life. This self-love is a luxury and a necessity for achieving success and fulfilment. You create a nurturing environment where growth and happiness can flourish by fostering a deep love and appreciation for yourself. Amidst life's complexities, it is easy to overlook the importance of self-love. When we neglect this foundational principle, we risk losing sight of our aspirations and dreams for genuine happiness and well-being. Indeed, to lead a genuinely satisfying life, we must first embrace and cherish all aspects of ourselves, trusting that life will reciprocate this love. Love is the bedrock of our inherent nature, shaping our identity and guiding our journey through life. It is essential, therefore, to cultivate a daily practice of self-love, as it holds the key to unlocking lasting happiness, inner peace, and improved health. How we speak to ourselves reflects our innermost feelings and influences the trajectory of our life's path. Therefore, nurturing self-love with gratitude is not just a choice but a transformative act that shapes our reality and enriches our existence.

Cherish your mistakes as valuable lessons, and strive to see the beauty in your body. By respecting and nurturing your body, you bolster the foundation of your self-love as you journey towards your aspirations. Establish attainable goals for nourishing eating habits and regular physical activity, recognising that your body is a sacred vessel deserving of care and reverence. Through this holistic approach to self-care, your capacity for love expands, infusing every aspect of your life with passion, clarity, and vitality. Embrace self-love as the catalyst for a vibrant, fulfilling existence where each day is adorned with hues of joy and abundance. Making self-love your priority will unlock the potential to lead a life brimming with happiness and purpose. Embrace the transformative power of self-love and watch your life unfold with boundless opportunities for growth and fulfilment. When you love yourself unconditionally, the possibilities are endless.

Finding satisfaction within

Achieving a profound sense of contentment begins with embracing ourselves wholeheartedly, acknowledging our essence, and embracing our unique qualities. When we reach a point of self-understanding and acceptance, profound tranquillity washes over us. We no longer engage in futile battles with self-doubt or lament over perceived shortcomings; instead, we liberate ourselves from tension and anxiety. The burden of striving to meet unrealistic expectations dissipates, allowing us to experience inner peace and profound self-satisfaction.

This fulfilment is only attainable when we extend genuine love and compassion towards ourselves. Embracing self-love entails minimal risk, and the rewards are immeasurable. Conversely, failing to cultivate self-love results in significant losses. Embracing self-love instils a mindset of acceptance, enabling us to navigate life's circumstances with grace and resilience. By embracing our power and taking ownership of our choices, we find contentment in the journey we traverse. The psychological impact of being satisfied with our lives cannot be overstated. It is a potent antidote to the stress and turmoil that often accompany human experience, fostering a sense of equilibrium and emotional well-being. Ultimately, by cultivating self-love and embracing our inherent worthiness, we pave the path towards a life characterised by profound satisfaction and fulfilment.

Buhlebethu S. Mpofu

Cultivating a healthy lifestyle

Embracing self-love empowers you to prioritise your body's well-being, ensuring it receives the essential components for vitality: adequate sleep, nourishing food, hydration, and regular exercise. While maintaining a healthy lifestyle poses challenges for many, nurturing self-love is a guiding force, propelling you towards achieving your life's aspirations. By loving yourself unconditionally, you infuse purpose into your daily endeavours, fostering a sense of motivation and direction. As you embark on this journey of self-love and healthy living, the positive outcomes of your lifestyle choices become increasingly evident. With newfound confidence, you eagerly embrace new challenges, emboldened by the resilience nurtured through self-love. Developing healthy habits extends beyond physical well-being; it encompasses gratitude, solitude, mindfulness, forgiveness, and self-assurance. Indeed, self-love is the cornerstone of healthy self-confidence—an unwavering belief in your worth, perspectives, and potential. With healthy self-esteem, failure is reframed as an opportunity for growth rather than a debilitating setback. Your sense of pride and assurance remains steadfast, bolstering your resolve to tackle daily tasks and pursue your aspirations with unwavering determination.

The profound impact of self-love extends beyond the realm of the mind; it shields you from the sting of loneliness and distress, fostering resilience in the face of life's challenges. Freed from the shackles of comparison and self-doubt, you embrace your unique journey, accepting its inherent difficulties with grace and optimism. Empowered by self-love, you approach life with an open heart and a willingness to explore new horizons, confident in your ability to navigate the complexities of existence with resilience and grace.

Fostering healthy self-esteem

Adopting self-love is the cornerstone of nurturing healthy self-esteem—a deep-seated belief in one's worth, ideas, and capabilities. With healthy self-esteem, failure is reframed as an opportunity for growth rather than a source of anguish. Your pride and self-assurance remain unwavering, grounded in a profound appreciation for your thoughts and abilities. Armed with this confidence, you approach your daily tasks and endeavours with steadfast determination, unencumbered by doubt or hesitation. Indeed, self-esteem plays a pivotal role in nurturing mental well-being and protecting against self-doubt and negativity. Central to this is cultivating an independent mind that trusts its judgments and perceptions of people and situations. This invaluable gift is bestowed upon those who wholeheartedly embrace self-love, fostering a robust sense of self-esteem that withstands the trials and tribulations of life.

By loving yourself, you lay the foundation for healthy self-esteem, empowering yourself to navigate life's challenges with resilience and grace. As you cultivate a deep-seated belief in your worth and capabilities, you unlock the potential to lead a life characterised by confidence, purpose, and fulfilment.

How do you heal yourself?

In our journey towards self-healing, we often find ourselves extending greater compassion and understanding to others than we do to ourselves. While we readily sympathise with the struggles of those around us, we struggle to offer ourselves the same level of forgiveness and kindness. We dwell on our mistakes, neglect to celebrate our victories, and harbour feelings of shame and unworthiness. Despite our innate desire for self-improvement, the relentless self-criticism we impose upon ourselves can erode our self-esteem and confidence. While constructive self-reflection is essential for personal growth, an excessive focus on self-criticism can hinder our progress and impede our well-being.

But why should we treat ourselves with kindness and compassion? Simply put, we deserve the same love and empathy we readily extend to others. Cultivating self-love is not a sign of laziness or complacency but rather a fundamental prerequisite for happiness and inner peace. When we harbour disappointment and unworthiness, our ability to experience genuine happiness becomes compromised. Likewise, shouldering the blame for every misstep only perpetuates feelings of guilt and self-doubt, trapping us in a cycle of self-imposed suffering. However, the path to liberation lies within us. We free ourselves from the shackles that bind our minds and souls by releasing guilt and shame. This newfound freedom empowers us to embrace love and kindness towards ourselves and others. In a world that often feels devoid of compassion, cultivating self-love becomes an act of radical kindness—an essential step towards creating a more compassionate and understanding society.

Ultimately, the ability to love others authentically stems from the capacity to love oneself. By learning to be kind to ourselves, we unlock the door to a deeper, more profound understanding of love—one that begins within and radiates outward, touching the lives of those around us. Here are some practical ways to start this journey of self-kindness:

Forgive Yourself

Carrying the weight of every mistake can feel like an overwhelming burden, suffocating us with guilt and self-blame. It is essential to remember that making mistakes is an inherent part of being human—it is okay to stumble and falter along the way. Instead of dwelling on past errors, we must release ourselves from self-condemnation and embrace forgiveness. By extending compassion and understanding to ourselves, we pave the way for healing and growth.

Accommodate Yourself

We are unique and remarkable with our strengths, weaknesses, beauty, and imperfections. Striving for perfection is an exercise in futility, as we are inherently flawed and multifaceted beings. Rather than attempting to conform to arbitrary standards or comparing ourselves to others, we must embrace our authenticity and celebrate our individuality. By accepting ourselves as we are, we unlock the power of self-acceptance and discover that we are inherently worthy, just as we are.

Congratulate Yourself

While it is natural to acknowledge and celebrate the achievements of others, we often neglect to extend the same courtesy to ourselves. No matter how small, every victory is worthy of celebration and recognition. Rather than downplaying our accomplishments, taking pride in our successes and acknowledging the hard work and effort that went into achieving them is essential. By cultivating a habit of self-congratulation, we bolster our self-esteem and sense of self-worth.

Taking Care of Yourself

In our fast-paced and demanding world, it is easy to prioritise work and external obligations over our well-being. However, neglecting our physical, mental, and emotional needs ultimately affects our health and happiness. It is crucial to carve out time for self-care, prioritising activities that nourish our bodies, minds, and spirits. Self-care is vital to maintaining balance and vitality, whether getting enough sleep, eating healthily, exercising regularly, or engaging in activities that bring us joy.

Treating Yourself with Kindness

Above all, we must treat ourselves with the same kindness, compassion, and respect we offer to a cherished friend or loved one. By becoming our most significant ally and advocate, we cultivate a deep sense of self-love and appreciation. When prioritising our well-being and happiness, we fill our hearts with joy and contentment, radiating positivity and love into our world.

11. Power Of Positive Confession

"Words are, of course, the most powerful drug used by mankind."
—Rudyard Kipling

Believe it or not, we engage in self-talk daily. Our minds are filled with continuous thoughts, many of which are harmful. Recognising the power of our thoughts and words and consciously focusing on the positive is crucial. While there are various methods for combating negative self-talk, positive confession is one of the most effective strategies. As human beings, our thoughts shape our reality, and self-love and forgiveness become elusive if we constantly dwell on negative beliefs. The adage "you are what you think" holds that our thoughts can mould our experiences and determine our outcomes. If we constantly berate ourselves with thoughts of inadequacy and failure, we hinder our potential for success and happiness. Therefore, it is essential to cultivate a habit of speaking positively to ourselves, affirming our worth and capabilities. Embracing positive confession may seem simplistic initially, and you may question its efficacy. However, the impact of affirming your greatness cannot be understated. By consistently reinforcing positive beliefs about yourself, you lay the groundwork for profound personal transformation.

So, how does positive confession work, and what are the benefits? Positive confession operates on the principle of cognitive restructuring, reshaping our beliefs and attitudes through repetitive affirmation. Repeating positive affirmations helps reshape the subconscious, building confidence, self-esteem, and inner strength. The benefits of positive confession are manifold. Not only does it enhance our self-esteem and self-confidence, but it also boosts our overall well-being and resilience in the face of adversity. By adopting a mindset of positivity and self-belief, we unlock our full potential and create a life filled with joy, abundance, and fulfilment. To make positive confession effective, consistency and intentionality are key. Set aside dedicated time each day to engage in positive affirmations and be mindful of the words you speak to yourself throughout the day. With practice and perseverance, positive confession will become second nature, empowering you to live a life of purpose and abundance.

How positive confession works

The effectiveness of positive confession is rooted in scientific evidence, dispelling any notions of it being reliant on mystical or spiritual forces. Positive affirmations and confessions find their basis in well-established psychological theories. The brain's remarkable plasticity enables it to adapt to various stimuli, shaping our thoughts and perceptions. But, our thoughts create mental images, whether positive or negative, which become increasingly vivid with repetition. Through consistent positive confession, we actively reshape these mental images, fostering a mindset of optimism and empowerment.

It is essential to recognise that while positive confession holds value, it is not a substitute for medical treatment, especially in cases of anxiety, depression, or other mental health conditions. If you are experiencing such challenges, it is imperative to seek professional medical assistance. Additionally, the efficacy of positive confession hinges on consistent practice. Just as one cannot become proficient at swimming solely through reading or owning swim gear, positive confession requires habitual practice to yield tangible results. However, it is essential to acknowledge that positive confession may not be equally effective for everyone, particularly individuals grappling with low self-esteem or mental health issues. Positive confession alone may prove insufficient in such cases, and seeking professional support is advisable. Attempting to employ positive confession without addressing underlying health concerns can lead to frustration and disappointment.

Understanding the limitations and potential of positive confession empowers individuals to make informed decisions about its role in their journey towards self-love and forgiveness. While it offers a valuable tool for fostering positivity and resilience, it is not a panacea and should be approached with mindfulness and discernment.

Benefits of positive confession

Positive confession is a powerful tool for effecting change in various aspects of life. Whether grappling with challenges or striving for personal growth, positive affirmations offer a pathway to transformation. Positive confessions can be a source of resilience and inner strength in times of adversity, such as when facing stress at work or within the family. They provide a means of reframing negative situations and cultivating a mindset of optimism and empowerment.

Moreover, positive confession proves invaluable during periods of self-reflection and personal development. Affirming positive beliefs about oneself can foster healing and renewal when seeking to bolster self-esteem, navigate through grief, or overcome life's setbacks. Similarly, positive confessions offer a means of sustaining momentum and striving for continuous improvement for individuals already thriving. Whether the goal is to cultivate new habits, enhance productivity, or foster kindness towards others, positive affirmations provide the mental framework necessary for success.

The benefits of positive confession are multifaceted and far-reaching. By consistently affirming positive beliefs and intentions, individuals can enhance their well-being, foster resilience, and cultivate a more fulfilling life. In the following sections, I will delve into positive confession's benefits, shedding light on its transformative power and potential to catalyse personal growth and self-discovery.

Positive confession makes you more positive

Embracing positive confessions can significantly enhance your positivity. Rather than succumbing to random negative thoughts, actively engaging in positive affirmations can uplift your mindset. By taking control of your thoughts and speech, you empower yourself to shape your behaviour positively. Your words hold immense power, influencing your actions and interactions with others. By starting each day with conscious declarations of kindness, you will naturally embody that positivity throughout your interactions.

Positive confession boosts your self-confidence

Positive confession catalyses bolstering self-confidence. Affirmations such as "I am a success" or "I will not fail" instil a sense of belief in oneself. Conversely, negative thoughts can sap energy and diminish self-esteem. By consistently embracing positive language, you elevate your self-esteem and confidence. Through the power of positive speech, you affirm your capabilities and potential, reinforcing the belief that you can manifest the reality you desire.

Positive confession helps to control negative expression

Positive confession is potent in subduing negative emotions such as anger, impatience, and frustration. Nothing seems to change initially, but consistent repetition makes the impact evident. Through continuous affirmation, you gradually gain control over your reactions. You will find yourself less prone to frustration, more capable of expressing anger rationally, and more patient in navigating situations and interactions with others.

Positive confession helps you to manage stress

As previously mentioned, affirming positive words enables you to effectively tame negative expressions, including anger. Negative expressions often serve as stressors, but by mastering their control, you can significantly reduce unnecessary stress. Moreover, should stress arise, your ability to manage it improves, consequently enhancing your overall well-being. Since stress can precipitate mental and physical breakdowns, speaking positively indirectly contributes to our overall health and wellness.

Positive confession helps to improve productivity

Positive confession acts as a powerful force in amplifying productivity. When you vocalise your commitment to having a successful day and delivering your best performance at work, you effectively program your mind to align with those aspirations, igniting a surge of motivation to realise them. Likewise, affirming the favourable outcome of your endeavours fuels your drive to exert maximum effort, ensuring that your work reaches its highest potential.

Positive confession helps in overcoming a bad habit

As bad habits are cultivated over time, so are good habits. Breaking a bad habit is a gradual process that requires sustained effort and unwavering determination. Awareness of your desire to overcome the habit is crucial, even amidst numerous distractions. This is where positive confession comes into play. By repeatedly affirming your commitment to relinquishing bad habits, you heighten your awareness of them, making it easier to overcome them. Do you find yourself disheartened by certain habits you possess? If so, practising positive confession can be transformative. Through consistent affirmation of positive change, you pave the way for shedding these detrimental habits over time.

Positive confession helps in reaching your goals

As mentioned, positive confession enhances your consciousness of your spoken words, making it crucial to consistently articulate your goals and dreams. This habit primes you to take actions aligned with achieving those aspirations, enabling you to surmount opposition with the power of positive thinking. By continually vocalising your targets, you fortify your resolve to attain them. However, the benefits of positive confession extend far beyond this initial impact. Integrating positive confession into your life may uncover numerous other advantages that propel you forward. Understanding these benefits is only the first step. To harness positive confession's potential, you must learn how to wield it effectively.

Many individuals dismiss the efficacy of positive confession because they have to grasp its full scope. However, you're poised to transcend this limitation as you delve into the intricacies of making positive confession genuinely effective. Stay tuned, for shortly, and you will uncover the strategies that unlock the transformative power of positive confession.

What are the steps to make positive confessions effective?

Positive confession is vital to self-love, offering a pathway to personal growth and empowerment. However, its effectiveness hinges on how it is wielded. It is essential to distinguish positive confession from wishful thinking, as they differ significantly in their impact. Positive confession is grounded in intention and action, rooted in the belief that affirming one's desires with clarity and conviction can lead to tangible results. Unlike wishful thinking, which lacks substance and purpose, positive confession is a proactive practice that fosters accountability and commitment to achieving one's goals.

To harness the full potential of positive confession, consider the following tips:

Continual Practice

Like any other skill, cultivating a habit of positive affirmations requires regular practice and dedication. Merely uttering positive statements occasionally doesn't yield significant results. To combat negative thoughts effectively, one must actively engage in positive thinking. Regularly affirming positive statements enables you to shape your thought patterns intentionally. Our minds focus most on what we contemplate frequently, necessitating consistent positive affirmations to counteract negativity.

Embrace Optimism

While vocalising affirmations may initially feel contrived, persistence is key. It is easy to feel tempted to dismiss the practice as ineffective, but persisting is crucial. Scepticism toward positive thinking can hinder its effectiveness, demanding a conscious decision to suspend doubt. Although results won't manifest overnight, exercising patience is essential to acclimate to practice.

Verbalise or Internalise

Whether to vocalise affirmations aloud or internally is a personal preference. Psychologists suggest that verbalising affirmations may initially have a greater impact. Placing written affirmations strategically around your living space, such as on sticky notes, can be constant reminders. Alternatively, a mobile application facilitates easy access to affirmations throughout the day.

Action Reinforces Affirmation

Affirmations serve as a precursor to action, yet action is indispensable for tangible results. Mere verbalisation won't suffice; action is imperative. If, for instance, you affirm a desire to make pizza, the dish won't materialise until you engage in the necessary steps. Positive affirmations pave the way for attitude shifts, but tangible actions solidify change. Small gestures embody the newfound positivity, like smiling at a colleague or extending an invitation.

Live in the Present

It is crucial to distinguish between positive affirmation and goal setting. Affirmations aim to reshape entrenched thought patterns, fostering confidence in current capabilities. Unlike goals, which necessitate effort and time, affirmations focus on present affirmations rather than future achievements. They serve to reframe existing beliefs and attitudes, fostering immediate change.

Grounded in Reality

For positive affirmations to wield maximum effectiveness, they must be tailored to specific attributes and attainable improvements within oneself. While change is possible, some aspects are more amenable to transformation than others. Positive affirmations may fall short if they centre on statements that lack personal conviction. For instance, if dissatisfaction with body shape prompts affirmations geared towards exercise, the reality may not reflect immediate physical changes. Nonetheless, consistent exercise yields health benefits, warranting a shift in focus towards appreciating bodily function and committing to its maintenance. Furthermore, directing affirmations towards inherent strengths and virtues fosters a transformative self-perception. Embracing one's unique qualities reframes self-assessment, mitigating frustration and self-criticism when desired changes do not materialise immediately. Everyone possesses distinctive talents and attributes; accentuating these strengths through affirmations fosters a more positive self-image. By prioritising self-affirmation, individuals cultivate resilience and self-acceptance, transcending the limitations of unattainable expectations.

In summary, positive confession emerges as a powerful instrument in fostering self-love. The pervasive influence of negative thoughts often fuels self-criticism and self-loathing. Overcoming these detrimental patterns necessitates the cultivation of positive affirmations as a habitual practice. Through consistent positive confession, one can infuse their inner dialogue with affirming sentiments, paving the way for a healthier mindset. Moreover, positive confession catalyses bolstering confidence and managing negative emotions and stressors effectively. However, it is crucial to recognise that positive confession must be complemented by tangible actions to yield tangible results. By integrating positive affirmation into your daily routine, you journey towards self-love and inner harmony.

Though seemingly simplistic, the impact of positive confession resonates profoundly. Its transformative potential cannot be overstated, offering a beacon of hope amidst the complexities of self-discovery and personal growth. Embrace the practice of positive confession, for within its simplicity lies the profound ability to cultivate a profound love for oneself.

12. Grasping The Mindfulness and Meditation Advantage

"Within you, there is a stillness and a sanctuary to which you can retreat at any time and be yourself."
—*Hermann Hesse*

Mindfulness and meditation serve as essential pathways to untangle the complexities of the mind, fostering clarity and tranquillity amidst life's chaos. While closely intertwined, they maintain distinct identities, each offering its virtues. It is crucial to grasp their nuances and embrace their harmonious coexistence to fully appreciate their transformative power.

What is mindfulness?

Mindfulness embodies a profound state of awareness characterised by its non-elaborative, non-judgmental nature, firmly rooted in the present moment. This space embraces every thought, feeling, and emotion without reservation. Through meticulous, non-judgmental observation of the present moment, mindfulness emerges, reshaping our relationship with life's unfolding events and experiences. As a transformative lifestyle trait, mindfulness diminishes reactivity and cultivates a sense of contentment. Consider a scenario during meditation where distractions abound, hindering focus on the breath. Amidst these distractions, an inner voice questions this inability to concentrate. Mindfulness practice enables us to intimately engage with this voice, unravelling its origins and assessing its significance. Through consistent mindfulness training, we equip ourselves to recognise, release, and revisit this voice at will, reclaiming mastery over our mental landscape.

Why is mindfulness different from our default mode?

Our minds are often cluttered with a multitude of thoughts on various issues. This busy mindset contrasts sharply with mindfulness, which demands an unrestrained focus on the present moment. Cultivating steady, uncluttered, and non-reactive attention is a departure from our usual way of operating. Many of us function on autopilot, unaware of our experiences and missing out on the sights, sounds, smells, and interpersonal connections we could enjoy. Although we may appear alert and present, our minds are often disengaged and preoccupied with past regrets or plans, which may be repetitive or inconsequential upon closer examination. When events unfold, our instinctive reaction is to rush to conclusions and make instant judgments, often from a limited perspective that fails to consider the entire picture, thereby restricting our options and creating problems. Mindfulness, however, helps us remain present and grants us a degree of control over our actions and detrimental, repetitive thought patterns. It allows us to understand a situation better and respond in a skilful, measured manner.

In our daily lives, a myriad of thoughts on various topics tends to clutter our minds incessantly. This bustling mental state starkly contrasts the serene focus demanded by mindfulness, which necessitates unwavering attention to the present moment. Cultivating a composed and undistracted mindset, free from reactive impulses, requires a departure from our habitual mode of operation. We often navigate life on autopilot, oblivious to the richness of our sensory experiences and the potential for meaningful interpersonal connections. Despite appearing alert and engaged, our minds frequently wander, ensnared by reflections on the past or projections into the future, many of which prove to be repetitive or inconsequential upon closer examination.

When confronted with unfolding events, our natural inclination is to hastily form judgments, often without considering the broader context. This limits our perspectives and exacerbates problems. Mindfulness is a guiding beacon, anchoring us in the present moment and giving us agency over our actions and detrimental thought patterns. It empowers us to discern a clearer understanding of our circumstances and respond with discernment and grace.

Various techniques facilitate the practice of mindfulness, catering to diverse preferences and lifestyles. These encompass:

- Seated, walking, standing, and moving meditation, offering flexibility in accommodating individual preferences and physical capabilities.

- Incorporating brief pauses into daily activities, infusing moments of mindfulness amidst the hustle and bustle of everyday life.

- Integrating mindfulness into compatible pursuits like yoga or sports enhances physical and mental well-being.

- Engaging in breathing exercises to anchor awareness in the present moment and cultivate a sense of inner calm.

- Embracing guided imagery, whether practised independently or with the guidance of a therapist, to deepen mindfulness and promote emotional healing and self-awareness.

Advantages of mindfulness practice

When engaging in meditation, it is essential not to fixate solely on the anticipated benefits, but rather to immerse oneself wholeheartedly in the practice. Mindfulness, characterised by its non-judgmental awareness of the present moment, yields many benefits. The benefits of practising mindfulness can be split into three:

Psychological Advantage

Stress: Recent studies have shown that mindfulness can significantly reduce anxiety. For instance, research involving university undergraduates found that those who scored well on mindfulness assessments experienced less physiological and psychological stress. Another study revealed that children with higher mindfulness levels coped better with the aftermath of a hurricane and were more resilient to post-traumatic stress disorder compared to their less mindful peers.

Happiness: Mindfulness plays a crucial role in enhancing our perceived happiness. Happiness is not merely a transient feeling but also offers protection against disease and death by fostering a positive mindset essential for maintaining health. For example, individuals with diabetes who practised mindfulness reported better control of their blood sugar levels and a significant increase in happiness. Similar improvements have been observed in people suffering from low self-esteem, anxiety, and depression.

Pain Control: The perception of pain is closely linked to one's mental state and can be exacerbated by stress. Incorporating mindfulness into therapy has been shown to improve the quality of life and reduce symptoms of depression in individuals with chronic pain.

Kindness: Mindfulness meditation enhances positive feelings and actions towards oneself and others. Metta, or loving-kindness meditation, starts with fostering kind thoughts and feelings toward oneself. This practice gradually extends to friends, acquaintances, and eventually, even to perceived adversaries, promoting forgiveness and compassion.

Addiction: Mindfulness helps individuals combat addiction by strengthening mental discipline and breaking dependencies. It increases self-awareness and control, enabling people with an addiction to recognise triggers and manage their emotions and impulses. Mindfulness also aids in redirecting attention and understanding the underlying motives behind addictive behaviours, helping to control cravings for substances like food and alcohol.

Cognitive Advantages

Memory: Mindfulness positively influences stress reduction, sleep quality, and memory enhancement. Improving mindfulness helps in recalling information more accurately. Studies have demonstrated that even a brief period of mindfulness practice, as short as three minutes, can improve memory performance. This has led researchers to suggest that mindfulness could reduce instances of false recall in eyewitness testimonies in court.

Creativity: Mindfulness boosts creativity by increasing focus levels. Individuals often emerge from mindfulness sessions, such as walking meditation or seated activities like yoga, with fresh ideas and innovative solutions. Additionally, mindfulness enhances the brain's capacity for additional cognitive processing by reducing its tendency to wander.

Attention Span: Mindfulness training helps to extend and strengthen focused attention. It improves endurance and concentration. Research has shown that individuals who regularly practice mindfulness meditation perform better on visual tasks and exhibit greater focus. Another study found that mindfulness can reverse brain patterns associated with mind wandering, worrying, and poor attention.

Physical Advantages

Genetic Benefits: Mindfulness enhances general health and improves telomerase activity, an enzyme that plays a key role in ageing and the body's age-related decline. Regular mindfulness practice could delay the ageing process, helping us maintain a youthful state for a more extended period.

Immune Function: A robust immune system is crucial for resisting infections and maintaining good health, particularly for immunocompromised individuals. Research has shown that women with early breast cancer who underwent mindfulness training experienced reduced stress, fatigue, and sleep disturbances, along with an improved immune response. This enhanced immunity aids in defending against carcinogens and other health threats.

Blood Pressure Control: Mindfulness can significantly reduce the strain on the heart, improving overall cardiovascular health. Genetic factors and diet can cause the heart to work harder as we age, increasing blood pressure. Mindfulness helps lower blood pressure by relaxing nerve signals that regulate heart function, blood vessel tension, and the fight-or-flight response, which can exacerbate stress-related alertness.

How to cultivate mindfulness

Here are a few popular techniques used to enhance mindfulness:

Mindfulness Meditation: This technique helps individuals become more aware of their thoughts, feelings, emotions, and bodily sensations. It involves focusing on the immediate environment, breathing, and other physical sensations without judgment.

Mindfulness-Based Stress Reduction (MBSR): Created by Jon Kabat-Zinn, MBSR helps practitioners manage stress, depression, and anxiety by fostering awareness of the present moment. It typically involves 26 hours of session time over eight weeks.

Mindfulness-Based Cognitive Therapy (MBCT): This approach combines meditation, mindfulness, and cognitive therapy to target negative thought patterns that contribute to depression. MBCT usually takes about eight weeks to show significant results.

Body Scan Meditation: This practice involves mentally scanning your body from head to toe, paying attention to any sensations, thoughts, or emotions that arise without forming judgments or conclusions about them.

Mindful Eating: This technique encourages people to focus on their actions, thoughts, and emotions while eating, free from distractions like TV or phones. It involves paying close attention to the taste, texture, and process of chewing and swallowing food.

Mindful Walking: Just as mindful eating encourages awareness, this method incorporates mindfulness into walking. It involves noting each step, the thoughts that arise, and the feelings experienced while walking. This is usually done in a quiet, open space but can be integrated into everyday walking with practice.

Resting Awareness: This technique involves observing your thoughts and feelings as they naturally arise while resting, without trying to control or change them. The aim is to allow thoughts to flow in and out without interference.

Visualisation: This practice helps individuals relax and become more mindful by imagining and visualising intangible qualities like happiness or love and exploring the various aspects of these feelings.

Mindfulness therapy techniques

During mindfulness meditation, it is usually easy for our minds to wander. If carried out under the guidance of an expert practitioner, they instruct participants to accept their wandering mind without feeling ashamed and teach them to note where their mind wanders. Meditation can be carried out with a timer if practising alone. You could start small (meditating for a few minutes) and gradually increase the length. Some types of therapy incorporate mindfulness:

Dialectical Behaviour Therapy: This assists individuals in breaking destructive thought patterns. A trained therapist usually carries out this therapy. Patients can work in a group with others to practice newly learned techniques. Dialectical Behaviour Therapy involves balancing acceptance with change and is effective in treating borderline personality, post-traumatic stress disorder, self-harm and suicidal thoughts. Mindfulness, effective interpersonal relations, distress tolerance and accepting emotions as they are. Acceptance does not translate to approval of the current situation, but we take it now. Acceptance, in this instance, is non-judgmental and non-evaluative.

Acceptance and Commitment Therapy: This also applies mindfulness as a key component. Acceptance and commitment therapy is about being honest about what bothers us and actively committing to a path of action. Mindfulness enables us to do this by linking acceptance and commitment. ACT is robust because it places you in charge of your thoughts, feelings, and memories. Mindfulness becomes an effective technique to help us see things more clearly.

Mindfulness Therapy for Couples: Mindfulness is a therapy technique that works for individuals and couples. It is uplifting for couples to practice mindfulness together, since it makes them more aware of their feelings and emotions directed toward one another. Couples can heal, grow, and solidify their bond. Mindfulness can help break previously buried feelings of resentment and bitterness, and this could give the relationship between couples a new lease on life.

Mindfulness Therapy for Depression: Mindfulness is a helpful tool to help depressives in their battle against depression. Mindfulness is combined with observation, acceptance, muscle relaxation and breathing relaxation. Mindfulness helps depressives in the active modification of one's feelings towards a desired direction.

Mindfulness Therapy for Anxiety: Anxiety levels of patients reduce significantly after mindfulness therapy. It also helps anxious individuals control their emotions and reduce their stress levels.

Mindfulness as a Cure for Insomnia: Through mindfulness therapy, insomniacs can access better sleep and break harmful sleep patterns. The effects of poor sleep include greater stress levels, increased hypertension, and impaired cognitive function. Through mindfulness therapy, insomniacs can navigate sleep disturbances.

Meditation manifests in various forms, with two main types:

Concentrative Meditation: This form of meditation directs all attention to a single point, effectively tuning out distractions. To attain a heightened state of being, the goal is to immerse oneself entirely in the chosen focal point, whether it is the breath, a specific word, or a mantra.

Mindfulness Meditation: Unlike concentrative meditation, mindfulness meditation addresses a range of issues, such as depression and anxiety. It fosters a state of being fully aware and engaged in the present moment, encouraging openness and acceptance of one's experiences.

Making mindfulness work for you requires consistent daily practice. The most widely practised form of mindfulness is meditation. Beginners can quickly learn the basics through resources like videos and podcasts. Regular practice allows them to meditate for extended periods without needing long breaks. In addition to mindfulness meditation, it is beneficial to incorporate other activities such as mindful walking, mindful eating, resting awareness, or physical exercises like yoga or sports. It is important to remember that your experience with mindfulness will vary from session to session. Some sessions will be easier, with minimal mind wandering, while others might be more challenging. Stay committed to the process and integrate mindfulness into your daily routine, as its benefits can be profoundly transformative.

13. Self-Acceptance; A Pathway to Self-Love and Forgiveness

"Stop hating yourself for everything you aren't and start loving yourself for everything you are."
—*Unknown*

Everyone makes mistakes, but learning from them, letting go, moving forward, and forgiving oneself is crucial for mental health, well-being, and personal growth. Accepting responsibility for your actions is the first and most challenging step toward self-forgiveness. If you have been making excuses or rationalising your behaviour, it is crucial to acknowledge your mistakes. You can avoid excessive remorse and guilt by taking responsibility and admitting to actions that may have negatively impacted others. Ignoring the critical step of reflecting on the disappointments and hurts you may have caused prevents proper recovery from emotional issues and pain.

Even when we attempt to be as flawless as possible, we might sometimes neglect the ones we love the most or fail to live up to the standards that others have set for us. Even if we have done everything possible, issues in our pasts and tales still need to be addressed. We must examine these concerns if we move forward with our heads held high. The truth is that low self-acceptance can hold you back in every aspect of your life. It impacts your self-esteem and can hinder you from attaining your full potential.

On the other hand, people who have a high level of self-acceptance are more tolerant of criticism. They see it as necessary and perfectly okay for them, but what is self-acceptance? Why are some people more accepting of themselves than others? How can you cultivate more of it, and how can it help you? Let's have a look.

What is self-acceptance?

Self-acceptance involves embracing all aspects of your personality precisely as they are, both the positive and the negative. This includes recognising and accepting both your physical attributes and mental characteristics. It means understanding that your appearance, intelligence, or actions do not solely determine your worth. Sadly, many individuals struggle with self-acceptance. They often believe that their looks, intellect, and self-discipline are inadequate. Even more distressingly, they may feel something is fundamentally wrong with them.

This mindset is exhausting and makes personal growth and change more complicated than it needs to be.

How lack of self-acceptance arises

The idea of low self-acceptance is an illusion. It is a construct of our minds. We've had these negative thoughts so often that they seem entirely true, but that doesn't make them real. The only place where this self-denial holds power and impacts you negatively is in your mind. Who is it that genuinely rejects you? Are you the one rejecting yourself? It is unlikely that anyone deliberately chooses to deny themselves. This self-rejection comes from a strange voice in your head, not from you. This inner voice tells you that you're not good enough, that you're too overweight, too skinny, unintelligent, or lazy. This is where the problem begins. If we mistake this voice for our own, we believe everything it says. We internalise all its criticisms about our character and abilities. As we know, every thought is linked to a feeling. So, when we trust this negative voice, we inevitably feel inferior.

True self-love is the result of this revolutionary realisation

You are set free when you realise that the negative voice in your head is not your own. You stop taking it seriously, no matter how much it complains, comments or devalues you. Pause and listen to that voice. Acknowledge that it is just a voice, and you can't predict what it will say next. Understand that you are the observer of this voice. This awareness creates a stronger connection with your true self. Genuine, profound self-acceptance is found in this understanding.

Why is it so hard to accept oneself?

Our caretakers shape and significantly influence how we perceive our place in the world from birth. This gives them considerable power over our self-perception and self-understanding. For instance, if your caregiver supported, loved, and accepted you, your self-acceptance will likely differ significantly from someone who experienced the opposite. When we start school, we are judged on our academic performance and how well we fit in with our peers. These experiences contribute to how we feel about ourselves and our level of self-acceptance. As we grow older, life circumstances, relationships, and the treatment we receive from others affect our ability to accept ourselves. So, what impact does self-acceptance have on your daily life?

Importance of self-acceptance

Research indicates that self-acceptance is crucial to overall mental health and well-being. Studies suggest a clear connection between low self-acceptance and mental illness. Conversely, low self-acceptance can harm various aspects of life, including daily functioning, career advancement, relationships, and overall quality of life.

Self-acceptance aids emotional regulation

A lack of self-acceptance can impact the area of your brain responsible for regulating emotions, potentially leading to increased anxiety, tension, or anger and resulting in mental imbalance and emotional outbursts. This deficiency in self-acceptance undermines your capacity for happiness and harms your psychological and emotional well-being. It keeps you fixated on your perceived flaws, perpetuating negative thoughts and emotions. Conversely, embracing self-acceptance can enhance your mood and shield you from the adverse effects of stress and despair. Trusting and acknowledging your feelings is essential, as self-acceptance fosters emotional resilience and promotes overall well-being.

Self-acceptance makes it easier to forgive oneself

Self-acceptance fosters a more positive, compassionate, and balanced self-perception. Dr Srini Pillay, a renowned expert from Harvard Medical School, emphasises the interconnectedness of acceptance and forgiveness. According to Dr. Pillay, our inability to accept and forgive ourselves can lead to internal conflict and fragmentation. The dichotomy between the part of us that seeks forgiveness and the part that needs forgiveness creates discord within ourselves. Self-acceptance bridges these conflicting aspects, enabling us to extend forgiveness to ourselves and move forward. This process is crucial for our well-being, as dwelling on past mistakes can perpetuate negative thoughts and emotions, trapping us in a cycle of self-criticism and regret.

Self-acceptance boosts your self-assurance

Self-acceptance empowers you with greater self-assurance by helping you understand that your perceived flaws do not define your worth. Feeling confident makes you more likely to act despite anxieties or doubts. Conversely, a lack of self-acceptance can hinder your progress and inhibit you from pursuing your goals. Self-acceptance allows you to acknowledge that failure does not define you; instead, it presents an opportunity for growth and learning on the path to success. With increased confidence, you can cultivate independence and make decisions autonomously, free from the need for external validation or approval. Embracing self-acceptance thus opens doors to personal growth, resilience, and empowerment.

Self-acceptance helps you be yourself

Lack of self-acceptance often leads to efforts to conceal or suppress one's true self, causing exhaustion. Embracing self-acceptance enables authenticity, irrespective of others' opinions. Embracing oneself brings freedom to be truly authentic.

Ways to practice self-acceptance

Let Go, Rise and accept the Unchangeable

Release your grip on the unchangeable aspects of life. Dwelling on what cannot be altered serves no purpose. Instead, consider composing a letter to yourself, acknowledging the necessity of letting go and welcoming the qualities you admire.

Identify your Strengths and Passions

Create a comprehensive list of activities and skills you excel at, such as sports, music, or art. Consistently engaging in these endeavours can bolster your confidence and self-esteem.

Silence your Inner Critic

It is tempting to heed negative self-talk and become your own harshest judge. When self-criticism arises, pause and reflect on how you would encourage a friend grappling with similar doubts.

Develop your Inner Circle

Cultivate a supportive inner circle of loved ones with whom you can share your deepest thoughts and experiences. Surrounding yourself with individuals who accept you unconditionally fosters a sense of belonging and acceptance. Additionally, consider seeking online support groups or forums to connect with like-minded individuals. Practising self-acceptance can be challenging, particularly when confronting aspects of oneself perceived as less than ideal. However, by embracing the present, putting the past into perspective, and valuing every aspect of your journey, you can foster a sense of self-love and resilience. In the forthcoming final chapter, we'll delve deeper into the significance of self-love and explore the psychology of shame.

14. The Role of Self-Love and the Psychology of Shame

"Shame is the lie someone told you about yourself."
— Anaïs Nin

Following harrowing experiences that shatter us, our perspective on life shifts. Without actively tending to our inner selves, we may fall into the belief that positivity has deserted us forever. Remarkably, with conscious effort, we can cultivate unconditional self-love. This self-love forms the bedrock of our existence, enabling us to find tranquillity and fulfil our life's purpose. Succumbing to negative emotions can cast us into a shadow of our true selves, fostering a sense of shame. Among emotions, shame is notoriously challenging to manage. Fortifying our self-esteem and nurturing self-love can shield us from unbearable thoughts and feelings as if we possess the entire universe within us. Furthermore, our life outcomes are intricately linked to how deeply we love, value, and honour ourselves. This self-love influences the jobs we pursue, the quality of our relationships, our health, and every facet of our lives.

Why is learning how to love yourself essential?

As you embark on the journey of self-love, a profound transformation unfolds. With each step towards embracing yourself, confidence blossoms, and your sense of self-worth deepens. This newfound strength emanates from within, propelling you into alignment with your true purpose and potential. Indeed, the relationship you cultivate with yourself is paramount—the foundation upon which all other connections are built. Extending kindness and compassion to others becomes challenging without genuine regard for your well-being. Why persist on a path that threatens to unravel your world and inflict mental and physical distress when the remedy lies within you? But loving yourself is the key. While the journey to self-love may present challenges, it is essential to emerge from the depths of doubt and insecurity, embracing a lifetime of gratitude for the blessings in your life.

Understanding of shame

Shame is a universal emotion, striking at the core of our being with its unbearable weight and paralysing grip. Nearly all of us have grappled with this intense feeling at some juncture. Moreover, shame often intertwines with various psychological disorders, exerting a profound impact on our mental well-being. Engaging in open dialogue and using practical tools is key to overcoming shame.

Walking over shame and self-judgment

Overcoming shame is a journey that unfolds gradually, akin to taking baby steps. It begins with the practice of affirming thoughts in the aftermath of mistakes. Through this conscious effort, we can address progressively ingrained habits of shame and self-judgment. Remember, it is never too late to rewire our brains and cultivate healthier patterns of thinking and being.

What is the difference between shame and remorse?

It is essential to differentiate our behaviour from our true selves. Shame often accompany harsh self-condemnation, leading us to believe we are inherently inadequate because of past events. In contrast, remorse involves acknowledging our mistakes without internalising them as a reflection of our worth. Unlike shame, which damages us, remorse allows for growth and healing.

How does the body physiologically process shame?

When we judge ourselves or face inappropriate shaming or judgment from others, our brain automatically shifts into a fight-or-flight response. This triggers the release of norepinephrine and cortisol, effectively shutting down brain cells and diverting resources towards survival pathways. In essence, subjecting ourselves to shame and judgment consumes significant energy and resources that could be directed towards enacting positive change.

Healing shame and restoring your self-esteem

Identify Your Triggers: Shame doesn't materialise out of thin air; specific events or circumstances often trigger it. You take the first step towards liberation by pinpointing what triggers your feelings of shame and paying attention to them. While this process isn't always straightforward—many of us bury our feelings using unhealthy coping mechanisms—conducting a thorough self-examination can reveal valuable insights and pave the way for healthier problem-solving.

Revisit Your Childhood: Our formative years significantly shape our perceptions of ourselves and the world. For some, childhood experiences of maltreatment or neglect may have instilled feelings of unworthiness and inadequacy. However, as adults with a broader perspective, we must recognise that our shame is not our fault. Understanding this can help loosen shame's grip on our present lives.

Cultivate Self-Compassion: Shame often makes extending kindness and understanding to ourselves challenging. Practicing self-compassion is crucial for progress. Research suggests that self-compassion can counteract the self-criticism that accompanies shame. Treat yourself with the same tenderness and care you would offer an innocent child, nurturing a sense of warmth and acceptance within.

Challenge Your Thoughts: Take charge of your mind by scrutinising and challenging unhelpful thoughts. Your task is to weaken shame's hold by reminding yourself of your worthiness and lovability. Challenge negative thoughts and replace them with affirmations of self-worth, gradually reshaping your inner narrative.

Be Open to Love from Others: Shame can erect barriers that hinder our ability to accept love and kindness from others. It is common to question the sincerity of others' affections and withhold trust due to lingering feelings of unworthiness. However, by actively working to shed these negative emotions, you can open yourself up to receiving love and appreciation from those who genuinely care. Embrace compliments without diminishing them and allow yourself to bask in the warmth of genuine affection, gradually allowing love to permeate your life more fully.

Ways to love yourself

The way individuals manage their emotions significantly impacts their overall well-being. Therefore, I would like to guide you through various methods for practising self-love and embracing yourself.

Forgive yourself for your mistakes

Many individuals encounter moments of shame, despair, and anger at various times. It is crucial to accept that being human means making mistakes. Forgiving yourself for past errors is one of the most beneficial things you can do. Consider your past a collection of experiences, learn from them, and move forward. By leaving behind old traumas and limiting beliefs, you enable yourself to live in a place of deep reverence and love.

Prioritise personal well-being

Primary care plays a vital role in learning how to love yourself. You thrive when you deeply nurture and connect with yourself. Self-love is a personal journey, so it is entirely appropriate to dedicate time each day to focus solely on your well-being. Make it a priority to drink water, consume nutrient-dense foods, exercise regularly, develop a meditation practice, and engage in activities that significantly benefit your physical and mental health.

Establish healthy boundaries

Your top priority in life should be to love yourself every blessed day. It is essential to prioritise your well-being before extending love to others. This isn't about being selfish but recognising that you come first, and everything else follows. You must learn to say 'no' when necessary to maintain healthy boundaries. By putting yourself first, you can avoid the risk of burnout and overwhelm. Remember, how you love and care for yourself sets the standard for how you love others.

Taking shame out of the driver's seat

If you have put forth your best effort but find yourself still struggling with overwhelming emotions, seeking the support of a therapist may be the most beneficial step forward. Therapy is a powerful remedy for overcoming shame, providing a pathway to confront fears through open and honest communication.

When does shame become detrimental?

Shame becomes detrimental when it shifts from a signal of misalignment with one's values to a persistent belief that one is fundamentally flawed or unworthy. At this point, instead of motivating constructive change, shame causes harm by affecting mental health, encouraging avoidance, and eroding self-esteem. When shame shifts from reflecting on actions to negatively defining one's identity, it ceases to be helpful and starts to impact well-being and behaviour in a limiting way.

Signs you have shame

Feeling unappreciated: This can manifest as a persistent sense that your efforts and contributions go unnoticed or are undervalued by others, leading to feelings of inadequacy or unimportance.

Feelings of rejection: Frequent or intense emotions stemming from perceived or actual rejection by others can lead to a diminished sense of self-worth and isolation.

Worrying about other people's opinion of you: Being overly preoccupied with how others perceive you, often resulting in anxiety about being judged or criticised and influencing your decisions and behaviours.

Hiding your thoughts and feelings from yourself because you feel embarrassed to share them: Concealing thoughts, emotions, or aspects of your identity due to fear of embarrassment, judgment, or rejection can lead to isolation and internal turmoil.

Having regrets: Feeling remorseful or disappointed about past actions or decisions, often accompanied by self-blame or a sense of inadequacy, can contribute to shame.

Being a perfectionist: Setting excessively high standards for yourself and experiencing distress or self-criticism when unable to meet these standards, which can amplify feelings of failure or inadequacy.

Making yourself inconspicuous: Avoiding attention or trying to blend into the background, possibly due to a fear of scrutiny or criticism, which may stem from a desire to avoid feelings of shame.

Feeling suspicious and feeling that others would take advantage of you: Being distrustful of others' intentions and anticipating that they will exploit or mistreat you can contribute to feelings of vulnerability and a guarded demeanour.

Feeling dishonourable and inadequate: Experiencing a pervasive sense of unworthiness or lacking integrity, possibly influenced by internalised criticism or societal expectations, leading to shame and self-doubt.

Wanting to change yourself to appease others: Feeling compelled to alter your behaviour, appearance, or identity to gain acceptance or approval from others, which can erode self-esteem and reinforce feelings of inadequacy.

Worrying about failure: Experiencing persistent anxiety or fear related to potential or perceived failures, which can undermine confidence and self-worth, contributing to feelings of shame when expectations are not met.

What is self-love?

You have likely heard the advice to forgive yourself for past mistakes and to treat yourself with kindness and compassion. Maybe you're wondering if you can get by without all this "self-love" talk. The truth is, you can manage, but you may never truly thrive. Self-love and self-compassion, though often used interchangeably, are distinct concepts. Self-love involves a deep appreciation for yourself, fostering growth in all physical, mental, and spiritual areas. Unlike self-compassion, which may be more situational, self-love is a steady practice that affirms your worth and reminds you that you deserve love and respect.

Conversely, self-compassion is an active practice that enables us to treat ourselves with kindness and understanding when faced with our shortcomings. Unlike self-compassion, which is more immediate, self-love requires cultivation over time. Ultimately, self-love plays a crucial role in helping us recover more swiftly from trauma while also equipping us to handle failure and feelings of embarrassment better.

Self-love consists of three essential elements:

Self-kindness: It involves recognising that you are human and bound to make mistakes, allowing you to forgive yourself for past missteps.

Mindfulness: It requires awareness of and consciously filtering out painful emotions that may lead to emotional distress, helping you avoid unnecessary suffering.

Common humanity: This is the understanding that certain challenges are part of the human experience and offer valuable lessons to prevent repeated mistakes. It also means acknowledging that you are not alone in your pain and that some circumstances are beyond your control.

How do you practice self-love? Since self-love involves embracing yourself fully and objectively, it includes several key actions:

- Acknowledging both your strengths and weaknesses.

- Accepting your imperfections as part of who you are.
- Validating your emotions and prioritising your mental health.
- Being patient with your growth journey.
- Learning from past mistakes and offering yourself forgiveness.
- Placing your own needs at the forefront of your life.

By nurturing these aspects, you build a foundation of true self-love.

What is NOT self-love?

Arrogance: Self-love does not involve belittling others or inflating your importance at the expense of those around you.

Selfishness: While self-love allows you to prioritise yourself, it doesn't mean disregarding others' needs or feelings. Consideration for others is still important.

Overindulgence: Self-love is not about giving in to every desire or craving. Excessive indulgence can lead to irresponsibility, as self-love requires balance and self-discipline, not letting your impulses take control.

If you have been following along, you will notice numerous advantages to practising self-love. Here are some of the most notable and impactful benefits:

Higher levels of satisfaction: Self-love allows us to truly appreciate ourselves, which helps us view the world more positively. We become more open to loving relationships with family and friends and take pride in our achievements and acts of kindness.

Greater happiness: Self-love fosters genuine happiness, helping us create positive outcomes and experience more fulfilment in life.

Reduced stress and anxiety: When you embrace self-love, you free yourself from unnecessary stress and anxiety. You learn to let go of self-criticism tied to minor failures or challenging circumstances.

Stronger motivation: Valuing yourself and recognising your worth inspires you to engage in new activities that foster personal growth. You will find yourself energised to try things like reading, exercising, or picking up new hobbies.

Increased extroversion: Self-love opens you up to love, improving your ability to connect and relate with others on a deeper level.

Greater wisdom: Self-love enables you to gain a deeper understanding of life's complexities through both positive and negative experiences.

Improved mood: If you have ever been weighed down by pain or negative emotions, self-love offers healing. It helps you move beyond criticism and embrace happiness more readily.

Enhanced health and personal growth: The outcome of self-love is growth. By prioritising your well-being and happiness, you prevent toxic people or relationships from entering your life. Additionally, engaging in small acts like learning a new language, picking up an instrument, eating well, or enjoying music can bring enlightenment and fulfilment to your life.

How to practice self-love

Practising self-love is a gradual journey that involves nurturing a positive relationship with yourself. Here's a detailed guide on how to cultivate self-love:

Self-Reflection: Take time to introspect and understand your likes, dislikes, strengths, and areas for growth. This self-awareness forms the foundation of self-love.

Positive Self-Talk: Practice affirmations and speak kindly to yourself. Replace self-criticism with words of encouragement and affirmation of your worth.

Setting Boundaries: Learn to say "no" to things that don't align with your values or goals. Setting boundaries protects your time, energy, and emotional well-being.

Avoiding Comparison: Resist the urge to compare yourself to others. Focus on your journey and celebrate your unique qualities and achievements.

Curating Social Media: Unfollow accounts that promote unrealistic standards or make you feel inadequate. Surround yourself with content that uplifts and inspires you.

Prioritising Self-Care: Prioritise your own needs first. Ensure you're well-rested and nourished, and engage in activities that bring you joy and relaxation.

Exploring Hobbies and New Experiences: Pursue activities that ignite your passion and creativity. Trying new things boosts self-esteem and expands your sense of self.

Physical Self-Acceptance: Appreciate your body for its strength and resilience. Look in the mirror with compassion and gratitude for everything your body allows you to do.

Mindfulness and Meditation: Engage in mindfulness and meditation to foster inner peace and clarity. Beginning your day with these practices creates a positive atmosphere for the day ahead.

Financial Awareness: Take charge of your financial well-being by understanding your finances, setting financial goals, and planning for your future security.

Challenging Societal Norms: Reject societal standards of beauty and success that don't align with your values. Define your measures of success and beauty.

Seeking Support: Don't hesitate to ask for help when needed. Surround yourself with supportive friends and family, or seek professional guidance if necessary. In conclusion, self-compassion benefits us greatly and allows us to escape the negative outcomes associated with a lack of self-love and self-acceptance.

Conclusion

As the final words of this journey echo within you, let them resonate deeply. Self-acceptance and self-love are not just concepts; they are the essence of our well-being, shaping our physical and mental landscapes. Consider the tapestry of your thoughts woven from the threads of self-perception. Until you repaint that portrait with hues of positivity and compassion, the treasures within you will remain obscured. Here lies the key: learning to love and forgive yourself is the alchemy that transmutes inner turmoil into serenity. It is the art of making peace with your true self and extending that peace to those around you. Picture a life illuminated by the glow of self-love—a life where every moment is infused with radiance and joy.

I have meticulously outlined steps throughout this journey, each a beacon lighting the path toward your enlightenment. These are not just words on a page, but tools forged to empower you. They are invitations to action, urging you to step boldly into the arena of your own life. So, as you bid farewell to these pages, let them not be an end but a beginning. Take hold of these insights and these strategies and wield them with intention. Embrace the transformative power they offer and watch your existence undergo a metamorphosis.

This is your moment—a turning point in your life story. Seize it with both hands and embark on self-discovery and fulfilment. With each step forward, know you are sculpting a future imbued with purpose, joy, and boundless possibility. This is your time to shine—so let your radiance illuminate the world.

Acknowledgements

This work represents more than words on a page—it is a culmination of effort, inspiration, and the support of incredible people who walked alongside me on this journey. To my family and close friends, your encouragement has been my anchor. Thank you for believing in my vision, even when self-doubt crept in. Your unwavering faith in me provided the strength I needed to see this project through. I am deeply grateful to those who shared their expertise and insights along the way. Whether through offering constructive feedback, brainstorming ideas, or simply lending an ear during moments of uncertainty, your input has been invaluable.

A special thank you to my parents, whose unwavering support and wisdom have been an enduring source of strength. Even when I doubted myself, your belief in me has been the guiding light that has kept me moving forward. You have shown me the value of perseverance, staying true to my values, and the profound beauty of giving my best in everything I do. Your love, encouragement, and the incredible example you have set have shaped me into the person I am today. This work reflects the many lessons you have instilled in me, and I am endlessly grateful for that. Thank you for always being my foundation, inspiration, and greatest champion. I also want to express my appreciation to those who did me wrong, as their actions became a source of motivation and growth. In their way, they inspired me to channel my energy into creating something meaningful.

Finally, I want to acknowledge the process—the late nights, the bursts of inspiration, and the moments of reflection that reminded me why I started. This journey has been as much about self-discovery as it has been about creating something meaningful for others. Thank you to everyone who has played a role in shaping this work. I hope it brings you the same inspiration and clarity that creating it brought me.

Thank You for Reading

Thank you for reading *Forgive, Love and Renew: A Guide to Unburdening the Heart*. Writing this book was a profoundly personal journey, but knowing it has reached your hands—and, hopefully, your heart—makes it all worthwhile. Your openness to exploring these ideas, embracing new perspectives, and walking this journey with me means more than ever. If this book inspired you to pause, reflect, or feel empowered, I am deeply grateful to have played a small part in your story.

As a new author, your feedback and support mean everything. If you enjoyed this book, please consider:

- Sharing it with someone who might benefit from it.
- Leaving a review to help others discover it.

If you'd like to stay connected, please check out my website, https://www.buhlebethumpofu.com/Home, for updates on future projects, personal reflections, and exclusive content. Thank you for being part of this journey. Together, we are creating a new narrative.

About the Author

If you benefited from this book, please consider posting an online review. Thank you in advance.

Buhlebethu Mpofu is a recent medical graduate who finds great joy in moments when her knowledge transforms into someone's healing. Between hospital shifts, she reads and writes, finding that words can heal in their own way. She sees her medical profession as caregiving, whether in scrubs or simply being present for others.

Visit the author's website at:
https://www.buhlebethumpofu.com/Home

Follow on X:
https://x.com/shortbread00

About the Publisher

Sulis International Press publishes select fiction and nonfiction in a variety of genres under four imprints:

- Riversong Books (fiction)
- Sulis Press (general nonfiction)
- Keledei Publications (spirituality)
- Sulis Academic Press (academic works)

For more, visit the website at
https://sulisinternational.com

Subscribe to the newsletter at
https://sulisinternational.com/subscribe/

Follow on social media
https://www.facebook.com/SulisInternational
https://x.com/Sulis_Intl
https://www.pinterest.com/Sulis_Intl/
https://www.instagram.com/sulis_international/

www.ingramcontent.com/pod-product-compliance
Lightning Source LLC
Chambersburg PA
CBHW032112090426
42743CB00007B/331